'An extraordinary tale' *Daily Tele~~~*

'A charm~ ~~~ ~~~ ~~~ ~~~ od
and an extraordinary account of what it takes to make it
on stage...I couldn't put it down'
Elaine Paige

'Wonderfully nostalgic and magical'
Easy Living

'A remarkable book...gripping, touching and
eye-opening...definitely one to savour and treasure'
Gloria Hunniford

'A charming and affecting memoir'
Sunday Express, Books of the Year

'A captivating story beautifully told...and what an inspiration
for anyone who dreams of a life on the stage'
Cat Deeley

'From the Blitz to Sadler's Wells, this is a charming portrait of
passion and dedication, set against the difficulties of war'
Woman & Home

'Dance historians will be as charmed by this sidelight on
dance as ambitious girls will be inspired by Lynne's description
of the dancer's life'
The Times

A DANCER IN WARTIME

Gillian Lynne is a British ballerina, dancer, actor, theatre director, television director and choreographer, best known for her iconic choreography of *Cats* and *The Phantom of the Opera*. She was born in Bromley, Kent, in 1926. At the age of ten she won a scholarship to the Royal Academy of Dancing, after which she joined the Cone Ripman School before being selected to join Molly Lake's Ballet Guild and Ninette de Valois's Sadler's Wells. As part of what would soon become the Royal Ballet, she was renowned for her portrayal of the Black Queen in de Valois's *Checkmate*, Queen of the Wilis in *Giselle*, the Lilac Fairy in *The Sleeping Beauty* and in roles created for her by Frederick Ashton and Robert Helpmann. Her film, television and stage credits include many long-running West End and Broadway shows, productions for the Royal Shakespeare Company, the English National Opera and *The Muppets*. She continues to produce television, film and stage productions and lives in London. *A Dancer in Wartime* was shortlisted for the Society for Theatre Research's Theatre Book Prize.

GILLIAN LYNNE

A Dancer in Wartime

The touching true story of a young girl's journey
from the Blitz to the Bright Lights

VINTAGE BOOKS
London

Published by Vintage 2012

2 4 6 8 10 9 7 5 3 1

Copyright © Gillian Lynne 2011

Gillian Lynne has asserted her right under the Copyright, Designs
and Patents Act 1988 to be identified as the author of this work

A CIP catalogue record for this book
is available from the British Library

ISBN 9780099555773

The Random House Group Limited supports The Forest Stewardship
Council (FSC®), the leading international forest certification
organisation. Our books carrying the FSC label are printed on FSC®
certified paper. FSC is the only forest certification scheme endorsed by
the leading environmental organisations, including Greenpeace. Our
paper procurement policy can be found at www.randomhouse.co.uk/
environment

MIX
Paper from
responsible sources
FSC® C016897

Typeset by Palimpsest Book Production Ltd, Falkirk, Stirlingshire
Printed and bound by CPI Group (UK) Ltd, Croydon, CR0 4YY

To my four great loves:

My Husband. Without whom this book would still be spidery writing in my notebooks and for whom my love is total and unconditional.

My Mother and Father. Who taught me almost everything – especially about giving.

The Theatre. I have never needed a drug, this magical world is it.

Contents

Prologue

To me a dancer's life is an amalgam of three crucial elements: the Impossible and the Spiritual all wrapped up with a ribbon of Passion.

The Passion must be there because this life is not for the faint-hearted. It makes the severe test of ability and stamina – the rugged day-to-day timetable of life – possible and pleasurable. A great athlete needs the same Passion. When this elixir (there is no other word for it) enters the veins, it lifts human beings who have chosen this extreme and often daunting life to a place where they can conquer the normal restrictions of their bodies and soar. When it flows freely through the veins the body feeds on it, greedily swallowing every last drop, and the muscles can achieve wonders and flourish. Then, to dance really well is glorious and the very toughness of it makes it so.

The Impossible is the constant battle with willpower. With dancing, there is often pain involved, and physical fatigue. It means saying no – to a large degree – to social normality and fun; it means adhering selfishly to a deliberately narrowed path. It means often not being understood by outsiders.

However, the Spiritual advantages are enormous. Being at one with the music, which plays a constantly intriguing part in a dancer's life, can lift the dancer to new realms and uncharted territory where all things can be attempted and discovered. Feeling at one with, and inhabiting and experimenting with, space is something other – something between your soul and the universe. It is private and occasionally extremely powerful, and certainly wonderful. It is a voyage of discovery led by your heart and not your technique. The Spiritual, if it is attained, can become a direct dialogue with the audience, who feel caressed by it and don't know why. It can help them, and thus you both thrive.

To dance can be a glorious experience and when you get the balance right it can lead you into a fascinating and endlessly interesting life.

It may have taken me a lifetime to understand this fully, but it all started when I was very young and entered into a lifelong commitment to exploring all the possibilities that dance tantalisingly offers. The pages that follow describe those very early years, of discovery, excitement, pain and dawning realisation. As I danced bigger roles; as I was exposed to the work of formidable choreographers and directors; as I began to work with acting stars; as I started to travel all over the world; as I learnt to embrace television and eventually began to choreograph and then direct my love affair with dance only intensified. It has enabled me to embrace many fields and help create some famous musicals that continue to play all over the world. It has even helped me to find my dear husband and discover that unconditional love can be a reality.

And for all this I have my mother to thank: for the priceless gift she led me towards and for the wonderful life she has watched over ever since, I offer up my most heartfelt thanks.

ONE

The Beginning
April–July 1939

My father, mother and me

THIS IS WHERE IT ALL began for me, the tragedy that has shaped my life, whose shadow I have spent a lifetime battling, but which continues to filter through, returning furtively at the most unexpected moments.

One morning I found my mother bent double, clearly in terrible pain and with blood all down her skirt, walking up and down the corridor of our bungalow in Sandford Road, Bromley.

'Darling, get Daddy, get Daddy.'

I ran to the telephone and, hand shaking, dialled my father's shop, George Pyrke and Sons. 'Daddy, please get an ambulance.'

My dearest mother was taken away and was very ill, for

what seemed like a long time, in hospital. She'd had an ectopic pregnancy – a very frightening thing. My father and I both feared losing her and we stood silently at the end of her iron hospital bed, trying to look hopeful, smiling wanly and willing her to feel our love. She was my darling mother, but she was also my best friend, taskmaster, helpmate and inspirational example.

By the end of June she had recovered enough that a plan was hatched for her and my father to go up to Coventry to stay with friends for a long weekend of recuperation and spoiling. We were part of a group of four families of friends: the Pyrkes, Thompsons, Turners and Rangecrofts, all with very successful and happy marriages. Only one family had any real money – Ed and Edith 'Fluffy' Turner. Ed was the brilliant designer of Triumph motorcycles so they lived outside Coventry near the great Daimler factories. They had no children, which was why their house was chosen for the grown-ups that weekend. The other three families all had children – the Thompsons had two daughters, Pat and Fay, I was the only child of the Pyrkes and the Rangecrofts had two sons, Laurence and John. We were a happy bunch.

The parents all went off to Coventry and we children, very excited at the thought of a discipline-free weekend, remained in Bromley at the Thompsons' house, with grandparents in charge. We had a host of adventures. Our own dramatics, our own mysteries, our own walks across the countryside, our own special trees for climbing – we created a wonderful world in which to entertain ourselves. As an only child I was in seventh heaven.

Up in Coventry that Saturday morning, the little gang of husbands and wives had gone out shopping; they had all had coffee together and then it was decided that the men would go home early to prepare cocktails and lunch, because four very attractive, spirited women – even though one of them was a little frail – wanted to do a little more shopping. Shopping over, the four women had started to make their way back to the house, which was on the outskirts of the city, when they suddenly realised they had forgotten to pick up the theatre tickets for that evening. Quickly they drove back to collect them. Now they were going to be late for lunch, and Edith, driving her baby Fiat with all four of them crammed in, put her foot down, probably not noticing that a very fine rain had started. On the long, avenue-like Kenilworth Road that leads out of Coventry, the little car skidded right into the path of the petrol tanker that was driving towards them on the other side of the road. All four women were thrown out of the Fiat, scattered several yards from each other by the force of the impact. If only they had skidded away from the lorry and into the grass verge, they might have been saved.

Back at the house the four men, with drinks all prepared, atmosphere bubbling as they waited for their wives, began to worry. After an hour they decided that my father and Ed would drive back along the road to Coventry to see if they'd broken down. Instead, they found a bloody scene filled with police, ambulances, medical personnel and newspaper reporters: the pageant of cruel road accidents. The other two men were called, they all had to identify their wives, then the three men with children back in Bromley set off home with their grim news.

In Bromley we children couldn't understand why we had been rushed inside in the middle of a wonderful game. We had been up a huge tree, our favourite climber. There was an unnatural quiet about the usually noisy house. We watched as, one by one, the grandparents disappeared and returned with reddened eyes. We weren't allowed to go to the windows and look out, since the press was camped in the front garden, and this made us even more ill at ease. We didn't resist being bundled off to bed early. Not all in the same bedroom as usual, we noted, but in separate rooms.

Downstairs, the hushed voices continued, with doors being very quietly opened and shut. I lay there with a feeling of dread flooding all over me. At around midnight the bedroom door slowly opened and in came my gentle, generous father . . . except the person now slowly sitting himself down on the bed was a wraith – his clothes seemed to hang from him and he was unable to control the shuddering tears that took over his body. Now I was really frightened. All children think of their parents as pillars of strength and wisdom, and to see your pillar crumble is a terrifying experience.

'Mummy is dead, darling – she and all the aunties have been killed in a terrible car crash.' He could say no more.

At that moment I heard an extraordinary sound: a sharp deep boom. It was very strange and to this day I cannot explain it, but in that instant I understood that my childhood had ceased. I took my father in my arms, cradling him and saying, 'Don't worry, Daddy, I'll look after you.'

My mother

TWO

Early Childhood

1926–1936

My mother and me

I WAS BORN ON 20 February 1926 to Leslie and Barbara Pyrke.
My father and his brother George ran the long-established
family business that provided removals, decorating, furniture and
funeral services (not an unusual combination in those days) in
Bromley. The rambling shop was at 147 High Street and had two
big picture windows with the entrance, quite elegant and handsome, in between. My grandfather had started the company, and
it was well thought of in the town as dependable and full of very
helpful salespeople. If customers were lucky, one of the brothers
would serve them. Both men were courteous and charming but,
more than that, they shared a kind of flirtatious magnetism that

meant customers felt happy and a little excited as they chose their lamps and curtains. If they were in the sad position of having to arrange a funeral for a family, Leslie (or Mick, as everyone called him) and George became caring uncles, guiding the grieving along with gentle kindness. So, all in all, George Pyrke and Sons was a stalwart of the town and did very well. No one in the family was rich, least of all the junior partner, my father, but no one was struggling either. Life was happy and fairly secure.

George Pyrke and Sons also owned a cottage in the Kentish seaside town of Birchington and our families took it in turns to spend summer holidays there. My first memories are of Birchington, a small, plain seaside town, but with a lovely central square – actually round – which housed a friendly, comfortable old pub overseeing all that was going on and a fantastic butcher whose delicious pork sausages were gobbled up with relish by our little family as soon as we arrived to spend our happy few weeks.

The cottage sat on a sliver of land squeezed between a golf course and the busy railway line from London to Margate. I loved it there: the excitement of the trains roaring past; the constant sound of Mummy's and Daddy's favourite singer Hutch crooning away on the squawking gramophone; the incredibly fresh air (I have yet to experience anything more intoxicating, except maybe the morning air in New Zealand); the arrival from time to time of children, especially little boys, from various other families.

Oh, what holidays we had! I rushed down to Epple Bay, where with reckless tomboy glee I explored rock pools with the boys, climbing over slippery boulders, working up a fantastic appetite and running across the bay, up the cobbled slope, along the road, up the gravelled and grassy lane towards the cottage where my mother was always ready at eleven o'clock with Bovril and bread-and-dripping. We would visit Herne Bay, Minnis Bay and the surprisingly magical town of Margate. One year, when Shirley Temple was all the rage, I persuaded Mummy to let me have my hair done in all-over curls like Shirley, and then I insisted on entering a children's talent competition on the pier at Margate, where I sang 'On the Good Ship Lollipop'. Mummy and Daddy were tentative about this but, in spite of having no voice at all, I won. Something must have been lurking.

Me at Birchington

By the time I was eight, it had become very clear that I suffered from some kind of excess of energy. So much so that I was a real pain to everybody. Nowadays I dare say I would have been labelled hyperactive and my diet would be scrutinised and a pill given, but back then the approach was quite different. My parents, at the end of their tether, took me to see our family general practitioner. I was quite a sickly child and he had seen me through a catalogue of childhood illnesses. He knew me as an invalid but not at my full, super-energetic best – I was nicknamed 'wriggle-bottom' at home. He observed me very closely as Mummy launched into a long speech about how frustrating she found my annoying symptons. The doctor fixed me with his highly intelligent beady eye, unobtrusively put on some music and said to my mother, 'Mrs Pyrke, I would like to have a word with you outside please. Young lady, you stay in here.'

Out they went and the minute they had gone I started to dance to the music, even going up on his desk because it seemed like a wonderful vantage point for jumping off from. What I hadn't noticed was that his door was one of those beautiful old glass ones with etched designs, through which the doctor and my mother were watching. Mummy told me afterwards that the doctor had said, 'There is no trouble with this child, Mrs Pyrke. She is a natural dancer – you must take her immediately to dance class.'

Mummy had always intended to let me learn to dance – most girls did in those days – but my vulnerability to passing germs had held her back. Now, however, she had our doctor's blessing. So the very next day we went to Miss Madeleine Sharp's class for young ladies in the ballroom of the Bell Hotel in Bromley.

The Bell Hotel was an important part of Bromley life and my parents, who were enthusiastic ballroom dancers, met friends there socially. But to me it was unexplored territory and full of possibilities. Mummy hurried me across the generous old marble-pillared foyer, up the wide magic staircase and, lo and behold, I entered the world that was to become my life. There was Madeleine Sharp – tall, slim and powerful, with a thin face, slightly beaked nose and wonderful probing eyes.

She asked us to sit down and watch, but I found this nigh on impossible because it was so exciting. The most wonderful little girl with tight brown curls, younger than me but clearly already a superb dancer, caught my eye. 'Mummy, I want to be like her,' I said immediately.

That child was Beryl Groom, who became the incomparable Dame Beryl Grey. Besides Beryl, there were eight other little girls, all of whom hung on Madeleine's every word and jumped to obey her instructions.

'Girls, listen to the music. Allow it to get into your body.'

I was immediately drawn into her aura. All great teachers must be part dictator, part charismatic star and must create an atmosphere in the classroom that will draw in the instinctive pupils so they can be changed into willing slaves. Miss

Sharp achieved all this and more; she made the word 'dance' come alive for us and her own imagination was so vivid that her classes were always an adventure, never a hard slog. She was capable of driving her charges relentlessly but her lessons were anything but the usual combination of technique, positions and syllabus.

At the end of my first glimpse of a proper dance class I was in a fever of excitement and longing to join in. As all the little girls were changing into their outdoor clothes, while mothers packed up ballet shoes and socks, Madeleine came over to Mummy and me and said, 'Right. Let's see what Jill can do.'

We began with the classic first rule for all dancers: How to hold the barre.

'Never grip it, dear,' she said firmly, 'rest your hand lightly on it. It is there to steady you, not as a lifeline. Turn your feet out – this must not be the feet only, but start in the hips so that your whole leg is turned out. Good. Now try to hold the knees together.

'Now point your foot, lift your leg, straight if you can. No, not with the shoulders hunched up with the effort. They must be down, and your back very straight and strong.'

And so Miss Sharp explored the possibilities of my untutored frame. Then she asked the pianist to play a lyrical piece of music and said, 'Jill, dear, let me see you run and enjoy yourself and see what the music tells you to do.'

I didn't know it at the time, but Madeleine Sharp was highly regarded and entry to her classes was quite competitive as a result. So Mummy must have been extremely nervous by now, especially as some of the other mothers had lingered to see how this new child was going to do. I got carried away with the music and flew around the room. After a minute or so Madeleine clapped her hands and I came to a halt in front of her, panting and looking up at her, full of hope. She put her arm round me, returned me to Mummy and said, 'I'd like to teach her very much. Can you come again on Friday?'

They exchanged a few more words but I didn't hear a thing, my head was too alive with the events of the afternoon and the thrilling new world before me. I was barely conscious of Mummy saying, 'Hurry up, darling. Let's get home and tell Daddy!' but as her voice woke me up I flung my arms round her and hung on for dear life.

When Daddy arrived home a little after us, we both spoke to him at once and soon he joined us in our euphoria. Our bungalow was a happy place to be that night, though I am sure that later, as one overexcited child was sent early to bed, serious discussion was had as to how my parents could afford these lessons.

Somehow the money was found and from then on I attended Madeleine's classes twice a week. Soon, the wonderful little girl I had seen, Beryl Groom, and I were dancing together. Our classes often included enacting little scenes Miss Sharp thought up for us – finding our way along a country path, discovering flowers and picking them – to make the hands and fingers find clarity. We also learnt skipping, character work with steps from a polonaise or mazurka and lovely *enchainements* (movements strung together that enable a dancer to develop fluidity and phrasing). Madeleine also set us mimes and movements to show we could act as well as dance.

At Christmas we performed in shows produced by Miss Sharp while in the summer we danced at garden parties, usually on the lawn of a large house, as sylphs, nymphs, dryads and flowers.

A Madeleine Sharp garden party; Beryl Grey (née Groom) is left,
I am saluting in the background

Besides ballet, once a week we had a tap class from a woman called Mary Cooke. Mary had stylish jet-black hair and she played the piano quite brilliantly, teaching us tap at the same time. She wore very tight black satin shorts and a white sleeveless tailored blouse, with blood-red lipstick and finger-nails. We thought she was very 'with it'. But the thing we noticed most about her was that when Mary showed us one of her tap steps and stopped sharply, saying 'Now you', although *she* had stopped, inexplicably her upper thighs had not and they happily kept on swaying for some time. This reduced us to helpless giggles.

On the more formal side, Madeleine Sharp put us through our Royal Academy of Dancing ballet exams. She felt that their solid technical rules would lay a bedrock in the bodies of her little girls (sadly there were no little boys) even if they did not ignite their passions. (She was more than capable of doing that.) We ploughed our way through Grades 1, 2 and 3, and the formality and discipline of the experience taught us inval-uable things: how to be ready for a special day, how to conquer our nerves, how to run the race on the right day at the right time. But Madeleine also taught us less tangible skills. Her dances and the themes for her shows were always well above average. She had an unusual imagination and we learnt early on not to be afraid of attempting anything, especially attempting a wide range of characters, including animals. (Once, Beryl and I did a pretty serious duet as 'two pigs in love, gentle and loving'. We found it quite difficult.) Some of her choreography was ahead of its time, too, as it fused classical with an element of modern dance and a hint of showbiz. The result was that we were well prepared for 'performance' techniques.

Beryl and I danced in everything, prattling to everyone and anyone about what we were learning. We talked a lot over the years about how lucky we were to have had such an instructive, disciplined first teacher, who taught us so much, especially about musicality, which is when a dancer reacts totally intuitively to the music, almost becoming part of its melody and rhythm.

We were so busy that sometimes it was a struggle to fit it all in. I had started at Bromley High School (we went to high school much younger in those days) and they did not like giving me time off for dancing. I was already having piano lessons and they thought that was quite enough 'art' for one child. At the end of my first year I won a junior cup for playing the piano, but then my first teacher, whom I had really liked, got ill and left, and her replacement was a cold, cruel woman who obviously did not take to me. She would hit my fingers while they were on the keys and constantly put me down. One day she pinched my right cheek, shaking it so hard that a tooth fell out and on to the keys. I picked up the bloodied tooth and ran home in tears, begging my parents to stop my piano lessons. They did not find another teacher for me, so my piano playing ended there and then. I was inconsolable as I adored music and wanted very much to become a pianist as well as a dancer. (What's more, in my profession as a choreographer and director it would have been invaluable.)

Whatever had gone on during the day, inspiring ballet or awful piano or boring school, whenever I came home along Sandford Road I would see Mummy waiting at the gate with love and welcome in her eyes. She always had a treat of some sort for me, a little fairy cake, an apple or a strange tomato with perhaps a baby one attached to it. At tea I would tell her all about my day, what I'd found difficult and what I'd sailed through, then would come the moment when she would lift the tea things off the table and say to me, 'Right, darling, practise.' It was the same every day.

I would run to my bedroom, scramble into the pair of black knickers and the little black tunic Mummy had made me, and pull on a pair of white knee-high socks and my pink ballet shoes. In our dining room I would hold on to a chair for a barre, with an encyclopaedia or heavy art book on it to steady it. I would repeat all the barre work that Madeleine had taught me, with Mummy watching like a hawk, patrolling up and down, watching, encouraging, urging me on. She would never miss a mistake and as she was so musical herself she was strict about my musical phrasing, even at the barre. She insisted I work flat out and if I got tired she would say, 'Right, deep breaths for a few moments then we'll try again.' And then, 'Darling, those feet look like cotton wool! Come on, let's do a lot of *tendus* [extending a pointed foot, straightening the leg and returning it sharply, like a little automaton] but come on, let me massage those toes. You do one foot and I'll do the other.' And we would sit on the carpet together pulling my feet into a better point and kneading them so the circulation was stimulated and would help us.

If she sensed low spirits in me she would say, 'Let's do that lovely *port de bras* with forward and back bend next,' as she knew I would do that well. My arms would be long by now and my back loose. To make a little present of it all, she would sing for me as if she were the pianist so I could let my passion for the whole process of dancing flow through my body. It was my mother, not any teacher, who taught me very early on that, as a dancer, it is precisely when you are tired that you find the reserves of strength that will build your stamina. During our sessions there was no such word as 'tired', but Mummy's was a loving discipline – I could see her joy when I did well. We were both as happy in that bungalow dining room as if we were on the stage at Sadler's Wells. We had the same strong purpose.

Throughout my childhood illness was never far away. I kept our doctor busy with everything it was possible to get: diphtheria, measles, chickenpox (twice), endless abscesses in my ears, bronchitis, and of course my tonsils and adenoids were taken out. I even had scarlet fever, which meant I had to be sent away to the Bromley Fever Hospital.

It's hard to imagine a more austere place. It was all grey-beige concrete, square and ugly, with long, charmless corridors, bare rooms and black iron bedsteads. As an only child who loved my parents deeply, I was suddenly spirited away to this rough, unyielding life and thrown into a rigid regimen. There was a high wall surrounding the hospital, but this didn't stop my intrepid parents, who simply brought a ladder. I would get a message that they were there and look wanly out of the window of the ward to see them waving.

Scarlet fever was very contagious and taken very seriously, and the ten quarantine weeks it took to recover from the illness seemed endless. The staff were strict, but perfectly kind, and once I had got over the initial horror of my plight my usual zest for life managed to struggle back up and I got on with getting well. While I was there, I also contracted a particular type of abscess, which apparently no one else had ever had, and the case was recorded in the medical journals of the time. As it wasn't the Fever Hospital's area, they struggled to get it to heal up.

Heavily bandaged round the neck, I was allowed to go into the convalescent unit for the last three weeks, where everyone – young, old, men, women, children – was flung together. My particular pal turned out to be what I thought was a middle-aged man, although in fact he can only have been in his twenties, who was very Cockney and taught me a lot of ribald songs, which I sang enthusiastically. This chap, with his eagerness to become a chorus master playing to the captive audience of our eclectic convalescent living room, was rather fun. He was slim and wiry with curly mousy brown hair and a lot of energy, even though he too was recovering from scarlet fever, and he relished the opportunity to pass on some of his Cockney humour. I took to it like a duck to water. I loved performing and learning his accent, so I got extra coaching – the others soon got bored and reverted to playing cards or reading.

'Alrigh', all you slackers I've got a new one for you this afternoon,' he would cry up and down the ward. 'Ere I learn' it when I was workin' on the docks – so roll up! Roll up! Anyone wanna learn me to'ally unique song? Nobody, eh? 'Cept my favourite little Jill. Her with the sodding great bandage round 'er neck. Alrigh', Jill, all the rest have given up on us, so let's see if we can give a rousing chorus with my ditty about me tiddler. One, two, three:

> *'Has anybody seen my tiddler?*
> *Tiddle-iddle-iddle-iddle-iddler.*
> *I brought him in with a whistle and a pin*
> *Oh how I laughed as I wheeled him in*
> *Coming home oh dear oh*
> *That naughty boy Diggy Diddler*
> *He stuck his finger in my honey pot*
> *And pinched pinched pinched my tiddler.'*

I worked at this jolly song really hard until he was pleased with my accent, by which time I too could have come straight from the docks.

On the wonderful day when I was allowed to leave, with my neck strapped up and a special silver paint on my wound, my parents collected me and drove their precious only child home. To their horror, they found out that she had become an out-and-out Cockney, who sang them one rather rude song after another in her happiness at seeing them. It took a long time to cure my groundbreaking abscess and even longer to throw off the Cockney accent, but eventually all traces of both disappeared.

It was wonderful to be home. We celebrated with one of our favourite activities: our family picnics. My mother was a great concocter of delicious picnics. In the spring, most Sundays when the weather was fair were spent in the country near Sevenoaks, Mummy having made up a picnic basket and Daddy

Gathering wild flowers

driving us to the woods, where we wandered among the waves and plateaux of bluebells, before sitting down on a rug for our lunch. Mummy would lay out a white cloth and get out her rabbit-and-bacon pies, her casseroles and little sweet fairy cakes, and we would eat it all up in quiet contentment. My homecoming picnic was perfect. Through everything – all the dancing and school and illnesses – foremost in my heart were my parents and our family, and I was as happy as anything to be with them again.

I was soon allowed back to the premises of the family firm in Bromley High Street, where I played with my cousins David and Molly on and through stacked mattresses, cushions, curtains and furniture. The shop to me was a place of endless interest and quite a bit of mischief. It was the ideal setting for hide and seek and we rolled about on top of and inside tunnels of mattresses, laughing and chattering until somebody heard us and came to stop our games. There were small offices hidden away in the midst of the furniture and at the back, and in the large yard were the removal vans ready to go out on their lumbering journeys.

Also out back were the black cars and hearses for funerals, because George Pyrke and Sons not only moved you while you were alive but also, furniture-less, on your last journey. Daddy had us enthralled with tales of the old days of the firm in his father's time, when the coffins were conveyed in horse-drawn carts. He told of winter disasters when the horses, carts and men – alive and dead – would end up sliding into the ditch. One time the poor horses were struggling up a very slippery road and they stumbled. The coffin fell off and, joyful at a last attempt at life, careered down the icy road, gaining speed as it went, chased hysterically by the sombrely dressed attendants who were praying that it wouldn't hit a kerbstone or tree and burst open in a last act of defiance.

Pyrke and Sons vans

THREE

The Dancing Starts in Earnest

1936–1940

Positions, please

WHEN I WAS TEN I won a scholarship to the Royal
Academy of Dancing. Not only was this encouraging
– Mummy and Daddy felt there might yet be talent in their
skinny little daughter – but it was a great help financially.
When my timetable at Miss Sharp's had escalated to three
classes a week, it was more than they could afford. They had
had to go to my grandfather on my mother's side for assistance.
My grandfather and I understood each other, and with a
generous heart he had wanted to contribute, but my parents
were proud and had not really liked asking such a big favour.
Now all those troubles were eased and a new professional – or

so it felt – phase in our lives began. At the RAD I would have two one-and-a-half-hour ballet classes a week from expert teachers, with no fees to pay at all.

I would travel by train with Mummy up to Victoria and then on the No. 52 bus to Holland Park Avenue and the headquarters of the Academy. The studio was a large room – very long – with mirrors all down both sides. It had been built at the back of a tall, elegant house, in what would have been the garden. It had linoleum on the floor and the ceiling was high. As you entered you saw a black grand piano at the far end, plus a couple of old settees and a square table. To us scholarship pupils the place was particularly hallowed ground and I felt very proud to be able to go and work there. At last things seemed serious. Here I was in a real working studio with music and barres and classes with very talented children, their mothers eagerly waiting outside the room for their little dancers' accounts of triumph or despair.

On the bus journeys home we'd climb to the top deck and, if we were lucky, find it empty. I would use the aisle and the backs of the seats to repeat my day's class, showing Mummy my *battements* and arabesques as we went up Holland Park Avenue, then down Park Lane towards Victoria. If anyone had looked in from an upstairs window he or she would have seen a thin child in full performance mode hurtling from one end of the bus to the other, with Mummy laughing and trying to calm me down but secretly enjoying it. When we reached the great concourse at Victoria station, with its fruit stalls and sweet shops, I would beg my mother to assuage my hunger with a chocolate biscuit and then, as I nibbled my reward, we would rush hand in hand to catch the train.

At my grandfather's house

I loved these weekly visits to London; it seemed to me that Mummy and I were on our own private charmed adventure. As I prattled away, my mother seemed more like my pal. Even then my competitive nature was breaking through and I felt that we were colluding to accomplish our wish for me to become a special leading dancer; to become something and someone that she and Daddy (who was the least ambitious man you could ever meet) would be proud of.

I was competitive but Mummy's ambition for me was real as well and was tied up with many things. It was not the ambition of a stage mother. She genuinely wanted the two of us to present Daddy with a gift of accomplishment from his only child. But I always thought there was something more to it than that. The artistry in her natural, very beautiful mezzo soprano voice had never been allowed to blossom professionally. I was an over-passionate, over-energetic and almost over-loving child and she wanted all this channelled into something that would amount to a solid vision for my life. Something I could hang on to. As it turned out, this desire was prescient.

She was also a skilled dancer herself. My parents' talent at ballroom meant they moved together as one. Every time they went to a party they would come into my bedroom to show me how they looked, and I would always beg, 'Let me see you dance, I want to see if Mummy's dress sways with her!' And off they would go, dancing up and down the corridor of the bungalow. If, as was often the case, I was recuperating and they didn't want me to get up, they'd sway, incline and skim round my bed. I thought they were stars, performing just for me. And when Mummy sang for me – which she often did as I badgered her to – I was ecstatic. If, however, there were friends of my parents to dinner, or a little party for grown-ups and children, and she sang as she was always asked to, I behaved disgracefully and sulked as I stalked out of the room. I didn't want to share her gift with anyone because I felt it belonged only to our little family or, worse, only to me.

*

With Daddy

When my mother died in the summer of 1939, my father was left a broken man. In my feverish desire to care for him I had to push aside the doom-filled thoughts that were constantly with me. They felt like black clouds that had too much density and they overwhelmed me. I missed Mummy with a terrible pain. My best friend and protector was gone but this all had to be hidden – I was *not* going to add to my father's despair.

I was completely numb at her funeral. After the crash it had been decided not to let any of the children say goodbye to their mothers as they had been so cruelly disfigured. The last time I had hugged my darling mother it had been so joyful; she had recovered from her long and painful ectopic pregnancy and was off to be fêted in Coventry by the close-knit group of friends who so dearly loved her. She knew I would have fun with the other children down in Bromley so we had pulled each other's legs about the adventures to come and the whole scene had been happy and glowing. Now there she was, lying so close – with only a piece of wood between us – yet so impossibly far. All I wanted to do was to snuggle up to her and bury myself in her warmth. It was hard for me to come to terms with the fact that in that coffin lay only a cold, broken body. I felt panicky, as if a huge void was about to swallow me up. All around me were relatives – near and far – and family friends; some I knew, some I didn't, all swapping memories of this charismatic woman. The church and wake were full of this love but I couldn't bring myself to join in. I was desperate not to let Daddy down and it was such a dreadful sadness that I put it for ever to the back of my brain.

In the following weeks and months, Daddy's way of trying to help me was constantly to plan things for us to do. Sometimes he took us out to restaurants, thinking the excitement and buzz would distract me and do both of us good. Unfortunately, because he wanted to make it special, he often picked places with a piano and unerringly the pianist would pick one of the songs my mother had sung so beautifully. Result: desolated father with tears pouring down his cheeks; embarrassed daughter trying to help father to hide his grief. Of course this was the opposite of what Daddy had hoped for from these outings. However, some of his other darling attempts did succeed, albeit in a roundabout way.

I had long been having riding lessons and now we often rode together, which worked well. We both felt good on horseback and he was such an elegant rider that I felt very proud of him. Also, I managed, even in those difficult days, to make him laugh, often inadvertently. We used to ride bareback quite a lot and I was often overambitious – acting the daring cowboy only promptly to fall off. Once, I crashed head first into a bed of nettles, where I got stuck, feet waving in the air, face reddening rapidly from the stings. Even to a man as full of sorrow as my father this was a funny sight, once he realised I hadn't broken my neck.

Unhappy child

My father had fought in the First World War, been captured by the Germans and made a prisoner of war, during which he sustained a terrible injury to his left arm. The Germans and English created an exchange system for prisoners who were too badly injured to be any future use to either side. He was lucky enough to be sent to neutral Switzerland into the care of brilliant Swiss doctors. There, a very caring physician began the long process of stretching and strengthening all the muscles, sinews and tendons of his now badly withered arm. It always remained four inches shorter than his right arm, but he could use it effectively – and played a mean game of golf.

Lieutenant Leslie Pyrke, WWI

During the course of 1939 it became obvious that the country was going to have to fight another war. Only a couple of months after my mother's death and still in the grip of despair my father, like all ex-servicemen, was recalled to the Army. Although this left me totally bereft – my dear mother senselessly killed and my father called back into the Services – I was relieved for him because he had loved being a soldier and nothing else would have assuaged the terrible grief that he was trying daily to come to terms with. He loved being part of a group working towards a mutual goal (I inherited this love), he enjoyed discipline and being in uniform, and he became so busy and ultimately powerful as he defended our country that he was forced to banish his grief.

Clearly, since he would now be away, a home had to be found for me and many friends were very generous to Daddy in his quest to find somewhere I could be happy. At first a wonderful, large, friendly woman with big bosoms, sturdy hips, a lot of energy and the appropriate name of Mrs Kinder swept me up into the heart of her family in Keston, very near Bromley. I don't remember much about her children or husband because hers was the all-pervading personality, and that is what has stayed with me. That, and her rules about knickers.

One afternoon Mrs Kinder, eyes penetratingly fixed on me, energy blasting past me, said, 'Jill, have you changed your knickers today?'

'No, these knickers were put on clean this morning,' I replied.

Mrs Kinder blanched and said, 'No, darling, change immediately, we never wear the same pair of knickers all day. We change after lunch, put on clean ones and the dirty ones you take off are washed immediately and hung out to dry, ready for tomorrow.' I now own more knickers than anyone else I know and still sometimes have to fight the urge to rinse out a pair before I go to bed, ready for the next day.

The whole of England was a nervous wreck, wondering where on earth Mr Neville Chamberlain had landed us. It put us all on our mettle and the air was filled with expectancy more than fear, strangely enough.

When it was quite clear that we were going to be bombed by the Germans, the whole Kinder family – and I – spent hours cutting up strips of brown paper, which we then stuck in crosses on all the windows of the house to stop the glass falling out if it was smashed. To us – the young ones – it was an unusual and daring game. To be allowed to desecrate a window was fun and it felt very exciting – we understood it was important, not just idle messing about. Mrs Kinder's house was on the edge of the Common at Keston in the midst of fabulous ferns and paths, little humpy mounds and ponds, so all this war prep seemed at odds with the irrepressible force of nature all around us. Somehow this heightened the sense of drama, the feeling of the unknown getting closer. However, it must have been very depressing for the grown-ups, especially as they had already lived through one world war.

At the end of 1939 – a momentous time for everyone in Britain, tragic and cruel for many people in Europe – Madeleine Sharp came to the rescue. Since Mummy's death there had been no one to take me up to London to continue my scholarship with the RAD. First Daddy and now Mrs Kinder had certainly had their hands full and I'd had no choice but to give up my hard-won place. My heart, already saddened, grew heavier and heavier missing my ballet classes. Miss Sharp had been cast very low by Mummy's accident. She had known her well and had been very fond of her. She suggested to my father that she should take me off to St Ives in Cornwall where Phyllis Bedells – the famous dance teacher and one of the original founders of the RAD – had evacuated her school. The little town had embraced her and the stalwart Trecarrell Hotel had offered to mother the girls and boys who had been wrenched away from their families. More than that, the hotel had offered up their ballroom as a studio for her classes. Madeleine had talked to Miss Bedells and wanted to take me, and a couple of other pupils, down to Cornwall for two weeks. My father, at his wits' end with all that was going on, quickly agreed, and a few days later off we went.

With Madeleine Sharp (second left), St Ives, Cornwall, 1939

The sands of St Ives have stayed rooted in my memory. Phyllis Bedells wound our Bromley posse round her little finger. We were all smitten and shared a single desire: to excel as dancers.

The sea air was strengthening and filled us with energy, the town was beautiful and full of lively unusual people and buildings, the beaches were made for little girls to run and skip and leap across in a series of *jetés* and we were as happy as could be at such a time of fear, danger and sadness. After our two precious weeks, enriched by Madeleine's care, Miss Bedells's talent and the treasures of Cornwall, we reluctantly returned home to Bromley, and the stresses and trauma of being close to London.

Of course, it wasn't long before what it meant to live through a war was clearly demonstrated to me: I was evacuated. To be exact, Bromley High School was evacuated, sent peremptorily off to the middle of Somerset. I was very unhappy. We were bundled into the train at Paddington with pathetic little suitcases, trailing our new gas masks, already feeling sick and lonely. Everything in our childish worlds was changing. I was luckier than most, I suppose. I'd already lost Mummy, and Daddy had been swallowed up by the Army, so I had developed defences in the face of uncertainty, but for many it was devastating to be forced away from their families. We arrived at an ugly former school in the middle of Somerset where the dormitories were created by lining up mattresses on the floor. Our teachers didn't seem best pleased either, faced with the prospect of being with their pupils twenty-four hours a day. As the news of the war grew more and more terrible, and here we were stuck in dull countryside with very few amenities and very little food, I became desperate – uprooted again and now with no dance or music at all to console me.

The news of the worsening situation across Europe came crackling through an old radio around which all the worried teachers would huddle, crying their eyes out. This was the final straw for me. There had been so many tears in the last year of my life and so little dancing or music. So I did the only thing I could, I ran away.

I walked for miles. I was not totally clear what I was doing and certainly had no idea where I was going, but it made me feel better to be doing something, rather than hanging about in the midst of the dire depression that had hit our poor little evacuated school.

Eventually I saw a welcoming brick farmhouse with steps up to its front door. I knocked frantically, suddenly realising how tired and hungry I was. The door opened to reveal a round, friendly face on top of a plump, aproned form who must have been shocked to find this bedraggled fourteen-year-old waif standing hopefully at the bottom of her steps. 'Hello,' I said, 'is it possible for me to have a cup of tea or a bowl of soup?'

The dear lady, as she turned out to be, asked no questions. She and her husband, who had now squeezed into the door frame beside her, accepted this outlandish request as if it were an everyday occurrence, and decided to let me calm down before they attempted to find out where I'd come from. They opened the door wider, shepherded me into the main room of the farmhouse, sat me down at the big wooden table, rumpled about on the lovely old black country stove and placed a bowl of steaming tomato soup in front of me.

I quickly perked up, thanks to the delicious hot food and their warmth. They gently asked who I was and where I had come from, and the whole sorrow of the last few months exploded in me. It must have been a big weep because, to their eternal credit (and my eternal shame, as I cannot now remember their names, or exactly where the farmhouse was), they wrapped me up, put me on the comfortable settee in the living room, covered me with an old rose-coloured eiderdown and told me they were going to let me stay there for a while. Soon, I was fast asleep.

The next day I rabbited on about my daddy and how proud I was of what he was doing, and I suppose they were then able to trace him and convey to him the fact that his lost daughter was safe and sound. A day later one of Daddy's sisters, Auntie Tossie, a prim, slim lady, but with the Pyrke twinkle in her eye, turned up to take me back to stay with her in her little house in Bromley. Somehow the authorities, probably at my father's request, had been kept out of the whole business.

Auntie Tossie, a fifty-five-year-old spinster, was almost but not quite handsome. She had a deep voice and a lot of energy – she was always positive and often very amusing. Despite her apparently narrow experience she was more than aware of what made most human beings tick. She was certainly worthy of some strong, witty, decent man, but showed absolutely no self-pity at not having found one. I felt entirely at ease with her.

Auntie Tossie quickly set about seeing if we could get me back to the dancing I was missing so frantically. After the whole running-away business, Daddy also understood I had to get back to dancing or I'd continue to be a nuisance to everyone.

Picture Post, which was not unlike the American magazine *Life*, had just run an article about a famous London dancing academy called the Cone Ripman school. Auntie Tossie had read the article and told my father about it. The RAD was based entirely on the art of classical ballet, whereas the Cone Ripman school covered classical and musical-theatre dance, acting and rehearsal class – learning the repertoire of the famous ballets and musicals – as well as giving a grounding in academic subjects. It was somewhere I could attend full time instead of continuing at Bromley High School. Of course, I absolutely loved the idea. Daddy contacted the school, which was adamant that I should audition for them. He responded proudly that I had had a scholarship to the Royal Academy of Dancing and that he felt they would probably want to take me.

Auntie Tossie obtained the keys to our little bungalow in Sandford Road, now sadly shuttered and closed up, and she and I went looking for my dance clothes and shoes. This visit wasn't easy because I had hardly been to our house since the car crash. As we walked along the road with its familiar houses to right and left, my spirits tumbled with every step. I couldn't help but remember all those times I'd come home from school and the moment when, after a slight bend in the road, I would see my eager, loving mother leaning out towards me over the gate; the sense of 'coming home' I felt, not for the little pretty bungalow but from the love emanating from her. I always ran the last few steps and instinctively I did it again now, somehow expecting her to be there. Instead, I waited outside the gate and house – so tidy they looked buttoned up – for Auntie Tossie to catch up, and asked her if she'd mind leading the way. The sight of the house, windows shut, no hint of happy carelessness anywhere, was too painful for me and I needed her to help cushion me a bit.

We entered quietly and halted. The rush of emotions trapped us and we could only stand still allowing them to swirl around us. Mummy's and Daddy's 'togetherness' was everywhere; the life we three had shared, the sheer neatness of our happy little family, ricocheted off the walls. Auntie Tossie, as of course she had to, launched into practicality. 'Jill, where were your practice clothes kept? Where were the shoes and how many are we looking for? Come on, darling!'

Pulling myself together, I wandered between all the different cupboards where Mummy had kept my clothes and shoes. The saddest moment of all was when I opened her wardrobe – all her clothes were there intact, and the unmistakable sense and smell of her filled my every breath.

Finally we found my class clothes and dance shoes and

tacitly, without discussion, we walked through every room of the bungalow one more time. Then we left, walking silently up the road. At Auntie's house we sat quietly and had a cup of tea. Eventually Auntie leapt up and washed everything we had found, except the ballet shoes.

Daddy managed to take a day away from his army responsibilities and up we went to London to Olive Ripman's studio in Baker Street for my audition. The school had two centres: the Cone part was above Lilly & Skinner's shoe shop on Oxford Street, the Ripman part on Baker Street. Olive Ripman, a shrewd, middle-aged, very classy woman whom I adored on sight, gave me a solo class consisting of barre work to warm me up and then *pliés*, *tendu*, *rond de jambes*, *fondu*, *développé à la seconde*, arabesques and *port de bras* – all regular exercises in the life of a ballet dancer. Then came centre work away from the barre, *pliés* again, more *port de bras*, pirouettes, *relevés*, attitudes, promenades, arabesques, jumps, *assemblé*, *fouettés*, and then she gave me a few improvisations to see what kind of theatre instinct I had. Daddy was allowed to watch and he must have been praying that I'd get through. After I had finished Olive pronounced, 'Lovely dancer's body; good line; we'll take her.'

I couldn't believe there could be any 'line' left after all I'd been through and no dancing to support it, but Daddy took me out to tea at the Lyons Corner House on Coventry Street to celebrate. The Corner Houses were important to many people during the war. They were sprawling palaces with different types of restaurants, halls and bars tucked away on many levels. Civilians, soldiers, lovers, workers, airmen, sailors, business moguls, ballet girls, shop workers all milled about, waiting, meeting, hugging, kissing, hoping, rushing and dawdling. The Coventry Street building was so alive that just to enter it was fun, even a little magical. In the middle was a very small beautifully decorated European café called Old Vienna – *the* venue for special occasions – and this is where Daddy took me. We had raisin buns and hot chocolate with cream on top (rationing had not kicked in too severely yet) and we sat dreaming up plans for the future. I think we both felt that somehow we were following the path that Mummy had wanted for her daughter. Seeing my father happy – even for this short while – was intoxicating. I felt like flying up and swinging from the small chandeliers that hung from the painted ceiling.

Daddy delivered me back to Auntie Tossie and told her about the day's momentous events. They spent some time trying to sort out how the travel to and from London every day would work. Then, after holding me very tight, Daddy returned to army life and my aunt persuaded me to go to bed. But I was too excited to sleep. A new life was about to begin.

Each day I travelled from Auntie Tossie's house to Bromley South Station, and thence to Victoria, on the bus up to Lilly & Skinner's famous Oxford Street shoe store, round the corner (with longing looks in the window) and up the stairs to the

Cone studios. During the day there would often be a journey to special classes in the Ripman studios – entirely more sober and serious – in Baker Street.

I was finally a proper, full-time part of a famous theatre school and from the first felt completely at home with the other pupils, male and female, since we had common goals and hopes. The horrors of Somerset soon faded, though I never forgot the generosity of my saviours in the farmhouse. At the Cone half of our school I met Malcolm Goddard, who would become my best friend of sixty years as well as a very good dancer and an excellent partner. Later, he also became a very talented choreographer and I performed a lot of his work in the theatre and in many television series and specials, often partnered by him.

The four principals, the three sisters Gracie, Valli and Lily Cone plus Olive (Ollie) Ripman, fulfilled quite different roles. Miss Gracie taught only ballet, according to the rules and style of the Royal Academy of Dancing, while Olive Ripman taught Greek dance as well as ballet and she favoured the Cecchetti system. Valli looked after the financial and administrative details and Lily was responsible for the pastoral side of things. Miss Gracie ruled the Cone school with a rod of iron. She invariably wore smart shoes and a well-cut grey tailored suit, and carried an expensive rather large handbag – way ahead of her time. No one messed with Miss Gracie and she never minced her words. She was totally honest and piercingly interested in your

*The principals of the Cone Ripman school: Gracie Cone
and Olive Ripman (centre) with Valli Cone and Lily
Cone either side*

whole persona, which became obvious every time she talked
or corrected you, and she expected the best out of anyone she
decided to teach. She was feared and respected by all of us
– a smile from Miss Gracie at the end of class sent you home
in a golden chariot. Miss (Olive) Ripman was a very different
talent but ruled the Ripman school with an equally strong
hand. She wore long graceful skirts in flowing, burgundy-
coloured materials and her hair was dark brown and short. She
had a strong, pliant personality and she was always tanned.
She loved to accompany class with a hand-held drum to beat
the time and she glowed as she willed us to be good. She was
just as fanatical as Miss Gracie but her methods were totally
different. I suspect Miss Ripman had a deeper insight into the

talents of her pupils but the two of them were remarkable, unusual and brave women. Their courage, in accepting responsibility for so many children at such a dangerous time, and their way of teaching us a craft of beauty among all the ugliness of the war, was inspirational. They not only shielded us from the horror but encouraged the thoughts and imaginings that would change our lives. No one who had the luck to be taught by them will ever forget them.

The days were long, the work tough and the journeys back to my aunt's house flew by. Auntie lived in a typical red-brick, beautifully neat suburban house with a long narrow garden at the back and a high hedge, which gave straight on to the embankment leading down to the railway. After returning from school I often squeezed through the gap in the hedge to sit on the bank and watch the trains whistling by. One day I watched in utter amazement the trains bringing the exhausted, injured and defeated soldiers of the British Expeditionary Force back from Dunkirk. These poor, battered young men, with their chalk-white faces and dazed eyes, were crammed into the carriages, some literally hanging out of the windows, gulping air. Their exodus from France had been horrendous, cruel and makeshift. The radio had been abuzz with stories of how they had staggered across the beaches as the German shells made havoc of their friends. Entering the water, they had pressed against the current and made their way towards anything that might float, grabbing on to nets, oars, ballast blocks, fishing tackle, shirts ripped off and thrown to them as their strength ebbed away in the water. Hands old and very young had yanked them, injuries and all, into the armada of ships of all sizes that had crossed the Channel to rescue them. Some had even hung on to string stretched across rafts – anything to get away from the death on the French beaches.

A few attempted a little wave from the train windows in reply to my frantic yelling, waving and dancing. I was trying to cheer them up, but most were in a state of bemused disbelief and shock. My own shock soon set in and translated itself into a deep sorrow and fear of what would become of them. I sat riveted to the railway bank. My aunt had trouble persuading me back to the house where she had already started preparing our high tea but, once she had, the emotional trauma of what I had seen morphed into greedy hunger. My loving aunt had rustled up lamb chops, mashed potatoes, grilled tomatoes and a little cabbage. Years later, I realised I must have gobbled up Tossie's rations that night as well as my own.

By now, the bombing in and around London was bad enough that no one thought it a good idea for children to stay there, certainly not if they had a chance of getting out. Most schools were desperately searching for places to establish themselves in the country. The Cone Ripman school had found premises at The Hallams in Surrey near Godalming and the school was duly packed off there. Because I didn't live in London itself I didn't go immediately with everyone else. When I finally did arrive, it all seemed incredible. The house was full of girls, older and younger, with only one purpose in life – to dance – and all our charismatic teachers had agreed to be evacuated with us, so there was a very dedicated atmosphere. And every night there was this extraordinary dance event.

The house itself was all dark wood with a main, high-ceilinged hall that had a minstrel gallery running round it on the second floor.

The Hallams at Shamley Green, Surrey

After my first supper there, I noticed that everyone was going towards the hall. Beautiful music playing from a gramophone pervaded every dark corner and shadowy arch of this space. I sat down very shyly next to a pillar and watched as one slender girl after another danced totally freely across and around the hall. A very friendly girl, Margaret, came up, squatted down beside me and said, 'Aren't you going to join in the dancing?'

I said, 'Oh, no, no, too shy, I think I'll just stay and watch.'

And Maggie, who was to become my best friend, said, 'All right, but just know that nobody will be looking at you, we all dance for ourselves. Don't be afraid.'

The wonderful mood was punctured from time to time by the ringing tones of our Matron, Bunny le Marchand, yelling, 'Form Three – Bed!' or 'Form Two – Bed now!' And children would quietly slip away.

Soon, I realised that indeed nobody was looking at anyone else, so I let the music propel me into the middle of the room and I started, very tentatively at first, to dance. I had no idea I was about to experience something very significant.

Before the ghastliness of my mother's death and the outbreak of war, I had been considered good and promising at dancing, but not a lot more than that. It was Beryl who was the brilliant one at Madeleine Sharp's school. But that night, as I gradually let myself go and gave myself up to the music, I was infused with a talent that I had not possessed before and I knew that I was going to become something special. My limbs felt more flexible. I was able to move my back anywhere I wanted it to go. I felt light, I felt fluid, I felt I could enter the music and become totally enmeshed with it. It felt like this huge advance in my abilities could only have come from my mother; it was as if she was sending me this generous gift. The feeling made me very happy and it took away a lot of the sadness that had been part of my everyday life since she had been killed. When it came to my turn to be called to bed I was reluctant to stop. There, in the shadows of one of the minstrel gallery pillars, was Maggie with a smile all over her face. 'I don't know why you were so nervous. I think you are going to be a very good dancer. See you tomorrow,' she said. And with that she hurried off.

As I called out goodnight after her, Matron admonished with: 'Quiet please, that new girl!' Despite being singled out in this way I followed Form One up to the dormitory that night feeling suddenly quite at home in this strange, makeshift but single-minded school. I was nervously excited about what lay ahead.

FOUR

From Pillar to Post

1940–1941

July 1941

O UR EVACUATED THEATRE SCHOOL WAS strong in dance but weak in all other parts of the curriculum. Knowing that dancing limbs have to be worked daily, our wonderful principals – affectionately dubbed the Misses Gracie, Lily, Valli and Ollie – only really had time to ensure that our physical lives remained constant. That was all that mattered to me too and The Hallams promised to be the perfect anti-dote to the misery of the past years. It wasn't to last, however, as the Army decided to station several platoons of soldiers in the middle of our all-girls school. It must have been very hard for testosterone-filled young men primed for battle to be confronted daily by nubile girls in tights, tunics and little else.

The Army's arrival meant our principals had to scour England for a new school and we were all packed off home again in the meantime. My stalwart Auntie Tossie was recovering from bad bronchitis and was not very well, so she and Daddy decided it would be best for me to stay with my mother's sister Bess and her husband Phillip Selby in Croydon. I was sad about this. Against all the odds, Tossie had fulfilled the role of guardian – to a grieving child in the most difficult of times – with love, knowledge, humour and, best of all, friendship. I would miss her. But being in Croydon would mean I would be able to see my father more often, which made me very happy.

My new friend from The Hallams, Maggie, was an orphan

Maggie at The Hallams

and was sent back to her guardian, an older lady who lived in the basement of one of those grand houses on Avenue Road, St John's Wood. The return home of the evacuated Hallams children exactly coincided with a savage intensification of the German bombing on south-east England.

Auntie Bess and Uncle Phil lived in a tall house on Addiscombe Road, East Croydon. Like Tossie's house, theirs also had a long narrow garden at the back, though it didn't lead on to the railway embankment in the same thrilling way. My aunt and uncle were heavily involved with the Concert Artistes Association, booking musical acts to go all over the country to entertain at formal dinners, business conferences and private parties. Auntie Bess was warm and, like my mother, possessed an intuitive rapport with people of all kinds. She was also very

Phil and Bess Selby, Bess dressed for swimming

bright and good at most things except cooking, which didn't really interest her. Phil was amusing and friendly but lazy – although he clearly loved my aunt, he actually did very little. I know my family was very critical of his lack of ambition and had hoped for a husband of better calibre for Bess, but their relationship worked for them and we got on well. My maternal grandparents lived ten minutes away and their wine cellar – my grandfather Tiger Hart's pride and joy – would prove a lifesaver in the latest onslaught.

It was July 1940 and my father, newly promoted to major, was now in charge of defence at Croydon aerodrome and had controversially closed Purley Way, the wide main road that ran alongside the runways, to improve security. The aerodrome had a glamorous history of private planes, film stars, politicians and record-breaking long-distance flights. Closing the road was controversial as it meant people could no longer pull on to the grass verges to gaze at all the amazing arrivals.

The bombing seemed to be getting worse each night, and Auntie Bess, Uncle Phil and I spent most evenings in our basement, or under the stairs, or on particularly heavy nights in a tin Anderson shelter across the road. Some light relief came in the form of a very sprightly, slim, older man who lived on the top floor of Auntie's house and joined us downstairs in the safety of the basement when the bombing became bad. He spent all his time holding a big cushion over his head, bent double like one of the seven dwarfs, saying, 'Don't be frightened, Jill, don't be frightened.' The awful thing was I wasn't frightened. It was the grown-ups' fear that I remember.

The Anderson shelter that we shared with several neighbours followed the national design of a rounded roof of corrugated iron bolted on to strong iron walls and had been sunk into a hole dug by the nice man who lived opposite. The idea behind the shelter was protection from shock and death, but also from being buried. You could have fought your way out of an Anderson with maybe some cuts or broken limbs, but you would not be buried under tons of rubble.

To enter it you went down five brick steps. Inside were two rough wooden benches – shelves, really – that ran along the walls. Depending on the number of people attempting to push into it – six was the limit – I either sat squashed like a sardine or, if I was lucky enough to be the only child, I was allowed to lie down. Naturally we all became quite close and it was here that I picked up the most important information about the war as the adult sardines shared the bulletins of the day. We soon got into a routine. Auntie and two other ladies always managed to make a thermos of tea, someone else had made flapjacks, the odd nip of whisky emerged on catastrophic nights. Somehow the tight-knit together-ness made the constant rain of horror from the skies tolerable.

The raids soon became a maddening part of everyday life. We took them less and less seriously, getting careless after hearing shattering thuds near us, yet always surviving. They meant hectic discussions: 'Sssh! Listen!' as we tried to estimate the size of the threat by means of the approaching rumble. 'Sounds like a big one' would be followed by a dash for the cupboard under the stairs. Otherwise it was just: 'I think this one is going past us.'

We would nonchalantly grab a biscuit from the kitchen before heading for the safest part of the basement and sometimes, in defiance, we dared to stay exactly where we were when we heard the distant thumps. However, these thumps were often followed by a lot of whistle-blowing, shouting and a massively huge crash very near to us indeed and then there would be an Olympic sprint towards the stairs. Uncle Phil had never moved so fast in his life and it would take him a long while to recover from the effort. Auntie Bess was a swimmer and therefore fitter: her childhood holidays had been spent in Brighton, where she regularly swam from pier to pier with the greatest of ease. Because their business was theatricals, Bess and Phil both had highly developed senses of humour and some of their comments about Hitler's ideas of grinding us into the dust were hilarious – and usually terrifically rude.

The news from all over the Continent was terrible. Back in May, Germany had invaded Belgium, Holland and Luxembourg. Holland had surrendered, so had Belgium. Norway had capitulated. Worst of all – and I had heard muttered conversations between my aunt and uncle about this – the German Army had entered Paris. But then the news had come that Neville Chamberlain had resigned and been replaced by Winston Churchill. Just to look at Churchill gave you courage and faith in the idea that somehow the tide of disaster would be turned. Then, in June, France surrendered.

Our tottery old radio had become our focal point. On it we listened to Winston Churchill's superb, intuitive speeches, inspiring everyone to keep going and find strength to carry on even though the news seemed to bring nothing but loss, death and lack of hope. There were also lighter moments, such as the much-loved 'Radio Doctor' who lectured us on the care of our bowels, warned us that problems could develop from eating bad food and gave us instant remedies: 'Remember that wonderful little brown-coated worker – the Prune – he should be with you as often as possible!' But every day on the train from East Croydon to Victoria my fellow passengers engaged in endless heated, uninformed conversations about the latest events. And one thing was clear, *no* thought of defeat or lack of hope ever occurred to Mr Churchill and people were fed by his brave words delivered with such ringing resolve. You could feel it in the streets and see it on people's faces – there was a purposefulness and a spring in the step. There was a feeling of belonging to a team, and this feeling became like our oxygen. To be needed is the most life-enhancing emotion any of us can experience and that's what we all felt.

I took the bus to the Croydon aerodrome often during this time but one day the doorbell rang and a young private stood there, at attention, frightening the three of us because we thought there must be bad news. The private said, 'Morning,

Miss. Major Pyrke has sent me to transport you to the aerodrome. When you're ready, Miss, I'll be waiting in the car.'

Any fourteen-year-old girl would have loved this moment and I certainly did! Kissing Auntie Bessie, I ran to the front gate and climbed into the car. The bus usually took a long, rather circuitous route to Croydon but in our car we were waved through several stop points and arrived at the front gates of the aerodrome what felt like minutes later. Daddy was waiting outside the cottage he had on the edge of the airstrip and I, acting as grown up as I could, thanked the private for delivering me so swiftly and ran at Daddy. I noticed how pale and thin he was. I didn't understand it at the time but we were in the middle of the Battle of Britain and his responsibilities were immense. We sat down in the cottage's tiny sitting room as his adjutant brought lemonade. It was a hot day and the drone of aircraft never stopped. I asked my father – actually I begged him – if I could go outside and watch the action. I lay in the long grass at a distance from the runway as the Spitfires staggered back to land, disgorging their crew who then lay inert beside them. Small armies of helpers rushed out with hot tea and sandwiches for the exhausted men, who were mostly too tired to eat and drink anyway. The helpers would try to coax them until a klaxon sounded, whereupon the pilots leapt straight back into the cockpits, the ground crew fell away and the aircraft took off again like dragonflies.

It was relentless. As soon as one plane landed another took off. Some had been hit by combat fire and came in awkwardly.

The fire engine had to scream towards the crippled aircraft and put out the flames. It looked devastating but Daddy had assured me that the Spitfires and Hurricanes they were flying were a worthy match for anything the Luftwaffe could throw at us. Our pilots had no idea I was there, as this choreography of war played out in front of my eyes. These young men, as they battled against the larger German Air Force, had become our symbols of hope. They seemed the only positive gleam in the ocean of black, bad news that surrounded us. It felt important, being near our brilliant knights like that. And they were very exciting in their leather flying jackets with ruffled hair falling over incredibly young faces. They were the epitome of glamour and it was the first time in my life I'd seen anything like that. I begged Daddy to take me

Major Leslie Pyrke

to the canteen, hoping to see some of them while they grabbed something to eat. The canteen was warm, the camaraderie, danger and urgency were intoxicating, and I was with the commander of the airport. I could not have felt more proud or special.

Not long after that momentous day the doorbell rang again at 241 Addiscombe Road and Auntie answered it in her usual matter-of-fact fashion. She thanked the messenger and closed the door. 'Jill, come downstairs, please. I have good news.' I rushed down and she informed me that it was time to return to school and my much-missed dancing lessons. At last our four intrepid Cone Ripman principals had found a large house in Leicestershire called Loddington Hall near East Norton.

My joy was tempered with a strong desire not to seem too excited at the thought of leaving my aunt's home. Although it had been lonely living with her and Uncle Phil, with not another teenager in sight, we'd shared many a laugh, especially during air raids, I was grateful for their generosity and I had grown very fond of them. But the bombing had escalated to an almost nightly event in London and when I contemplated the countryside of Leicestershire, the chance to get back to class and be with friends again, it was impossible not to feel a set of powerful springs in my feet. And perhaps my understudy parents would simply feel relief at not having to be responsible for their off-beat niece in such hazardous times.

My aunt conferred with various other parents about the

idea of sending me away again and the plan met with approval, relief and curiosity. I contacted Daddy and left a message for my good friend Maggie. All the occupants of the Anderson shelter were delighted with the news that I could get back to my dancing. Wild hopes were shared about young Jill embracing a ballerina's life in spite of the dreaded Luftwaffe droning over our little shelter. A feeling of warmth settled on Addiscombe Road: now we had a sense of purpose.

Two weeks later Daddy managed to accompany Auntie Bess and me to East Croydon station to catch the train to Victoria. He could not be away from the aerodrome for long so we clung to each other, hating to say goodbye, but I could feel how relieved he was that I was going to a safer place. Auntie and I then caught the bus to King's Cross and there was Maggie on the platform. I ran towards her and hugged her. We waited for everyone to arrive and eventually we all boarded the train from London to Market Harborough via Luton and Kettering.

I waved to Auntie Bess until the last minute, then joined the feverish buzz along the corridors. We had no idea what this Loddington Hall would be like but we eagerly anticipated the physical work – and pain – and the fulfilling joy that daily class gives a dancer's life. We wondered excitedly who would be teaching us, whether the pianists would be good, what other classes we would be taught and what the classrooms would be like.

I worried that the break in our training would have harmed my muscles and bones, and that the rapid improvement I had seen at The Hallams would have been wasted. However, the minute we disembarked and leapt into the bus waiting to take us to Loddington all anxiety left me and I joined in the hysterical anticipation. Very soon we would see the place that was to become our home. We turned the corner and there it was, huge and austere, a grey and white building spreading sideways rather than up, not very beautiful to look at, but through the large wrought-iron gates we also got a glimpse of lovely green slopes leading to a lake.

In all we were about fifty girls, aged between twelve and sixteen, at Loddington Hall. Some I knew from Cone Ripman but there were many new ones, too. We all crowded into the main hall while our teachers tried to sort out the dormitories. A few of us started looking through the rooms soon to be transformed into our dance studios. The commotion pervaded the house as we discovered more friends and new faces. The noise was unstoppable, the staff's attempts to quell it pointless.

I felt nervous as I was shown into my dormitory. Having been so rootless since Mummy's death, I was full of uncertainty. I knew that this dormitory would need to become a place for me to feel happy and secure. It was fairly bare. The beds were small and there were not many places to stow belongings. I looked around hopefully for Maggie. There was no sign of her but there were other friendly faces, all anxious as well, and my bed was near a window with a stunning view down to the lake. I was certain that we would all have games and adventures there.

Eventually, Maggie rushed in to see if I was settled and I rushed back to look at her dormitory, pleased it was not far down the long corridor. We were allowed out before supper and a gang of us from The Hallams – Sonia, Claudie, Maggie and I – with at least twenty other girls, charged out into the grounds to explore every path and mound and slope. In and out of the trees and bushes we went, and were pretty pleased with what we found.

A clanging bell called us all in to eat and we had our first taste of Loddington's meagre food. Our bread was tasteless white cardboard. Margarine replaced butter, a bad raspberry jam – and a thin scraping at that – was all we had to help the bread down. Lunch would be thin soup, sometimes with vegetables, and an occasional fish dish, while dinner was a stew or sometimes mince, with potatoes and cabbage. To round off the meal the staple dessert was spotted dick, but made with currants, not succulent raisins.

Loddington Hall was pretty stark, with few comforts. We had iron bedsteads, there was not a lot of warmth (the dance classes saved us – our blood was constantly stirred up), the food was terrible, we were miles from anywhere and the countryside was bleak rather than pretty. But this grey and white house suited our theatre school well. Its rooms held little charm but the large, paved terrace that ran the length of the house was a place of constant energy and life. Classes of all kinds took place on it: school (such as it was) at one end, acrobatics simultaneously at the other, teachers' consultations in the middle and pupils rushing through it all to get to their classes. Heavenly bedlam! We enjoyed every moment of it.

We were all particularly thrilled with one of the new pupils: a very young boy and an unusual addition. He was small and neat with blond wavy hair. He was utterly fascinating to all of us as he excelled in all types of dancing. He wore a little bright red cable-knit sweater over his black tights, with white socks and black shoes. His name was John Gilpin and he was to become one of the great *danseurs nobles* of British ballet. He would also become one of my closest friends.

Having been assigned our various classes, we began training in earnest. We limbered up before breakfast, then came essential ballet class. We had mus. com. – as we called musical comedy dancing – three times a week, acting, character and Greek dance class once a week and tap twice a week. Sadly, there was still very little schooling. My French was good but I never progressed beyond eighteen per cent for Mathematics.

Misses Gracie and Olive were somehow managing to keep a skeleton school going in London so they spent a lot of time travelling up and down. Much of our day-to-day teaching was therefore handed over to two marvellously inspiring ballet teachers, Marian Knight and Betty Davis, the women who now started to shape my life. I set out to try to be the best dancer in every class. My body was strong and the right shape, with very long slim arms and legs and a shorter torso. All of it responded to whatever Marian Knight and Betty Davis could throw at it. I had an overarched back, which was to give me trouble later on, but I would have killed for either of these women. So I worked like a fiend and began to improve rapidly.

Miss Knight drove me on ruthlessly – ruthless love is pretty much necessary in the dance world – but she loved my spirit. She would set the class an exercise at the barre: '*Fondu-développé devant* carry to the side, two *ronds de jambes en dehors* lift the leg and carry round to the back into arabesque and *penché*, return to fifth *en arrière*. Retire to fifth in front and a single pirouette *en dehors* finishing in fifth.' After she had answered any questions she would turn to me and bark, 'Jill Pyrke, from you I want splits in the *penché* and a double pirouette to finish.'

I would struggle hard to deliver exactly what she wanted. I worshipped her and she always demanded that little extra, usually in the form of determination. She was about my height – five foot four and a half – and her frame was narrow, stretched and firm. She wore tight skirts that came just below the knee and neat little jumpers, usually with short sleeves. She was clean-cut as a personality, too, and her willpower cut through any gathering of girls like a knife. But it was the wonderful, confidence-giving expectation of us that was really powerful and, as I've come to realise, essential in a good teacher.

Betty Davis was much softer as a teacher. She had a degree of mystery about her and cared more that we should feel the love for dance in the music than worry too much about technique. She helped us access our dancing 'souls'. We were blessed to have a pair of such different and remarkable teachers to guide us.

Dancing was paramount in our lives and anyway there was little to distract us: no going home to the bosom of our families, no bus or train journeys to get us to school, no cinemas or theatres to tantalise – we were totally focused. As a result, all but a few pupils made great leaps. This was wonderful but also dangerous for me. I was very ambitious. I wanted to make Daddy (and Mummy) proud of me and became desperate to be as near the top of the school as I possibly could.

Maggie and I could see that the teachers were particularly interested in us and I (not Maggie as she was of a much gentler nature altogether) began to feel horribly envious of anyone who could do things better. Our two wise head girls, Maureen and Nancy, noticed this. Both were beautiful – Maureen was dark and enigmatic, Nancy fair and tall. They dressed with style and in the dreary corridors of a boarding school in the middle of a war they were the epitome of chic. We all thought the world of them and their opinions, and longed to be invited to tea in their private room which, to us younger girls, was a place of unimaginable glamour.

Maggie and I knew Maureen and Nancy also thought very highly of us, as they seemed to look on us fondly no matter how naughty we were. So imagine how excited I was when, at last, the summons came.

They had a modest sitting room, painted a warm and happy

Jill, Brenda and Maggie at Loddington

combination of pale dove-grey and pink. A small settee and armchair nestled under a large window that overlooked the garden. 'Come in, Jill,' Nancy began. She beckoned towards the armchair. 'Please sit down. Actually, on second thoughts, perhaps it would be better if you stood.'

They then took it in turns to say they'd noticed envy developing in me, and this was unattractive and totally inappropriate as I was doing rather well and had no reason to be envious of anyone else.

'Envy will eat into your heart. And the heart should be kept warm, receptive and open if you wish to be a creative artist in future,' Maureen said.

I left feeling utterly dejected and slunk out into the grounds to wrestle with their words in private.

As painful as it was at the time, I was lucky to have had this invaluable lesson rammed down my throat so early on, especially by two people I so admired. I've carried their words with me ever since and if I ever feel envy creeping over me about anyone or anything, I try to observe, analyse and work hard to push myself up and beyond it.

In the little time we had off we either went roaming round the lake, tadpoling or bicycling. 'We' usually consisted of Julia, Diana, June Carter, June Ratcliffe, Claudie, tomboy Tilsa, Mags, me and our young star John Gilpin – an extraordinary mix of age, build and fortune, or lack of it, all sharing a passion for dancing. Often we would also meet up and go on adventures with lads from the nearby public school, Uppingham.

On one such occasion we were cycling hell for leather through the country lanes when the road abruptly turned into a steep hill. To our horror June Carter was going much too fast and we watched her lose control. She came off her bike violently and rolled over and over down the hill, crashing her head against a small white milestone. She lay there moaning in the sun, blood pouring out of her head. We rushed in to help but one of the Uppingham boys said, 'Don't touch her, we must just guard her.' Some of the gang raced off to get help. June was this crumpled pretty little girl – with her white skin, the red blood all over the side of her head and down her neck, and her agonised moaning growing fainter. We froze in helplessness and disbelief. Older people started arriving now, rushing from cottages and the nearby school. After what seemed ages an ambulance arrived. But by then our friend had lost too much blood. She died on the way to the hospital.

Suddenly the war – the reason we were all in this unfamiliar setting in the first place – loomed over us. Combined with this horror, so close to home and personal, our senses went into shock and we were enveloped in darkness. The school, usually so full of noise, became quietly sober. The police interviewed those of us who had been with June. For two days no work was even thought of.

We decided to make our own wreath for June's funeral. We all went out to collect wild flowers and John Gilpin and I, always hand in hand, roamed far and wide, collecting the best flowers we could find for our poor friend. Somehow we managed to create a wreath in the shape of a ballet shoe. When June was taken away in the casket for her burial the whole school turned out to say goodbye and as the ballet shoe wreath we had made for her was placed on the coffin we wept with pride, knowing our love would accompany her on the journey home.

It took time, but after June's death we did settle back to work, perhaps with extra will. It was as if we were trying to make huge leaps for her to make up for what she was missing. And while things might not have been easy at Loddington Hall, beyond its gates things were much, much worse. We had to spend many nights in the cellars as the German blanket bombing of Britain unfolded. Loddington was along the path of the Nazi planes as they started their ferocious attack on the industrial heartland of England. Coventry, very near us, was bombed ruthlessly in the process and lost its proud cathedral. We heard the planes' muted and extended roar as they flew over and back, and we spent more nights trying to sleep on our benches in the cellar than in our beds. It taught us stamina, that's for sure, and while I wouldn't wish it on anyone, it was incredibly good training for the theatre.

Our progress as performers improved despite everything. Having several classes a day from very good, very demanding and caring teachers meant we were developing strengths and facilities that enabled us to fulfil the messages sent to our bodies from our brains. I was beginning to be able to talk to my body in specific places and it obeyed. In dancing, there is a process of isolating brain from muscle, which means you can intensify instructions so that your body responds with extra strength, resulting, for example, in the ability to send a rifle fire to your upper arm and shoulder while keeping your hand and wrist soft and gentle.

Our teachers were as strict as hell but we worshipped the ground they walked on. If Miss Gracie took our ballet classes we shook with fear, but found the challenge and standards she demanded absolutely compelling, which is not to say there weren't also moments of mischief. She often perched on the edge of a slim wooden chair and sat with her legs apart in a perfect *plié à la seconde*. Her smart grey skirt would ride up and be stretched tight across her thighs, revealing the dangling lacy crotch of her camiknickers. We loved this unwitting impropriety and no one ever told Miss Gracie – if they had they would have been lynched.

We started to learn ballet repertoire – the roles from famous classical ballets every dancer must be familiar with and which form the backbone of all great companies, both in terms of training and performances. During a season of performances a company will perform single ballets (known as 'full-lengthers') on some nights and on others a series of selections taken from great ballets, usually three one-act sections. This same combin-ation will hold whether the company is performing in its own theatre or on tour and, of course, it will also determine a company's training for that season. So learning this repertoire was to be our future. We all longed to be part of a ballet company and that would mean fighting each other for it, as most of the girls at the school had the same goal. A very few – the plump ones or the short-legged or large-hipped ones – were sensibly using dance to bolster their acting talents, but for the most part serious dance was our collective obsession.

These classes took place in the large rehearsal room, which had been the ballroom. Miss Knight or Miss Gracie or Mrs Ripman would unfold the great choreographic work of past masters to us and we responded with reverence and willpower. We were extra-ordinarily attentive. We knew that it was these classes that would show our teachers who really had the elusive and indefinable *it*.

We all let our hair down, even our brilliant classical dancer

Book-learning as well as footwork must be acquired; one of the classes at work in ballet dress.

WHEN the great evacuation took place at the beginning of the war two enterprising and well-known London dancing schools decided to try and keep going by establishing themselves and their pupils in a country retreat. Thus the Cone-Ripman School of Dancing came an amalgamated enterprise (though both Miss Grace Cone and Mrs. Olive Ripman's schools in London continue to have separate existences) at Loddington Hall, Leicestershire, seat of Lord Alberton. Some eighty students of three different groups, juniors from ten to fourteen; seniors from fourteen to sixteen; and full-course students from sixteen upwards are established there. Two resident schoolmistresses supervise the ordinary education of the girls, and there are four resident dancing mistresses and, of course, a general manager, hospital nurse and domestic staff. Full-time students have six hours' dancing a day, and the younger children have four lessons on general subjects and two dancing lessons. Ballet, work, Eurhythmics, tap and ballroom dancing are all taught. There is one boy in the school—little John Gilpin—and does he have a good time! Fire-fighting and gas-mask drill are, of course, obligatory. Dancing dress is worn most of the time so as to save the girls having to change continually. (PHOTOGRAPHS BY PICTORIAL PRESS.)

Sur les pointes at the blackboard; fourteen-year-old Tilsa Stubbs combines dance practise with other studies.

A peep into the dormitory while some of the girls are getting ready for a ballet rehearsal.

Right; Rosemary Henry tying the ribbons of her ballet shoes. Knots must be on the inside of the ankle and no ends must show.

The Sketch *ran a piece on our Loddington school. I can be seen bottom left, brushing my hair*

PHOTOGRAPH BY HUMPHREY SPENDER

BALLERINA'S GOOD-NIGHT.

This dancing study with a young ballerina sur les pointes looking up at a group of coryphées posed on the steps of a fine curved staircase might well be a new ballet divertissement. It is actually a real-life picture of Joan Bower, one of the pupils of the Cone-Ripman School of Dancing, practising a ballet pose in front of six other admiring students before going to bed. The dancing school left London on the outbreak of war and is installed at Luddington Hall, the seat of Lord Alleton. Other photographs of the ballerinas in their lovely country retreat are given on following pages.

I am second from the bottom on the stairs

77

Rehearsing Puck

John, in musical comedy and tap classes. Playing her drum with abandon, Olive Ripman invoked classical Greece for us and opened up a whole new world. I also loved acting class which, if you were primarily training for 'the ballet', happened once a week for two hours. Our teacher, Miss Harris, was young, beautiful and blonde with an excitable imagination. She presented us with an eclectic mixture of plays to study and also vividly introduced us to poetry. Hers was a rich class indeed and her inspiring ideas about playing Puck, a part I was proud to be given, flooded back to me years later when I played the role in BBC Television's production of *A Midsummer Night's Dream*.

Towards Christmas there were rumours that some of us would swell the cast of *Dick Whittington* at the Arts Theatre Cambridge for the coming 1940–1 Christmas season. The director and choreographer visited our school and we had to dance and sing for them. When the names of the pupils to go to Cambridge were announced, mine was among them. I was to be one of eight 'London Kiddies' and we were all sent off in a bus with Auntie Gwynne, our matron, plus dance shoes, practice clothes, a few pieces of ordinary clothing and our gas masks. The 'kiddies' all stayed in local digs. We shared bedrooms and a rather inviting living room. I was determined that we should have a bowl of fruit (apples being about all we could get) or flowers on the mantelshelf over the fire to make it feel more homely.

We rehearsed our hearts out and loved being in a real theatre. When the director started putting all the elements of the show together – changing the staging of his actors to create the best effects with the lighting, running songs through with the orchestra, making sure the actors used the scenery and inhabited the stage fully, yelling when their timing was off – we learned to sit as quiet as mice in the stalls until it was our turn. We fell about at the comic's antics and adored our female lead. We 'kiddies' sang the finale 'Meet the Sun Halfway', which was a lot cheerier than the programme note from Air Raid Protection warning us to 'remember always to bring your gas mask with you'. Life was very different from Loddington Hall and the Leicestershire countryside but that made it all the more exciting to us first-timers.

Back in our digs, things weren't so thrilling. Auntie Gwynne had never approved of my left-handedness and now she finally really had me in her grip. She started insisting that I eat right-handed. Each meal was agony as I followed the food round my plate. At one high tea before going to the theatre I was listlessly chasing peas when Auntie Gwynne pronounced, 'We are all going to sit here until Jill has eaten every pea.' The others glowered hatefully at me and wriggled around impatiently but Maggie looked at me kindly and proclaimed, 'Don't worry, Jill. We can wait happily. Can't we, girls?' Good old Mags.

When the first actual performance of *Dick Whittington* began, our childlike fervour exploded with such unstoppable noise that the older actors banged on our walls and told us to: 'Shut Up! Others are working on stage!' This was an essential theatre lesson learnt the hard way and early on – how it should be. Even so, the dressing room crackled with such sparks of excitement that I was amazed Auntie Gwynne didn't ignite. But on stage, *we* did – our untrained voices rang out, our legs shot up in high kicks and our smiles dazzled. All our classes and discipline unleashed a youthful energy that flooded over the pit and into the auditorium, lifting everything up as we chorused towards the sun.

We returned to school as the snowdrops were blissfully reigning over the banks and hedgerows of our grounds. I went out early in the freezing cold to pick some for Miss Knight, who had become my absolute heroine. With nervous pleasure I arranged them in a small tumbler by her setting at the breakfast table and waited anxiously for her to notice. 'Oh, how lovely!' she said as she sat down. She held the flowers in front of her and sniffed the scent, looking all round the table. 'Whoever picked these for me must have been frozen. It was a very nice thought.'

After breakfast she turned and said quietly to me, 'You picked these snowdrops for me, Jill, didn't you?' My huge smile confirmed her suspicions and she added, 'Thank you, darling.'

After this exquisite encounter my will to work exploded and I tied a picture of Tamara Toumanova, the beautiful Russian 'baby ballerina', to the end of my bed and read absolutely everything I could lay my hands on about the world of ballet. I spent hours with my feet trapped under a chest of drawers so they were forced to point better and I rushed through our ghastly breakfasts to get to class early so I could have space to practise and catch up on all I'd missed while we'd been in Cambridge.

Then, in March 1941 the Leicester Repertory Company contacted the school to say they were presenting Dodie Smith's play *Dear Octopus* and they needed a girl to play Scrap Kenton, a sad little girl who had lost her mother, and did the school have anyone suitable? Well, not only was I suitable, I *was* that little girl! I got the part and was shipped off, with a chaperone, for the journey to Leicester.

Dear Octopus was already a famous play and had been an instant success when it opened at the Queen's Theatre on Shaftesbury Avenue in September 1938. The reviews had been glowing and the original cast had been full of stellar, and soon to be stellar, names like Marie Tempest, Angela Baddeley and the young John Gielgud. Dodie Smith was one of those clever writers who could make you chuckle even as the tears snaked down your cheeks. Her plays were warm, real and often very comic, with plenty for the actors to get their teeth into. I felt lucky to be chosen to star in such a gem.

Although being involved in a play was a totally new experience for me, the dancer's way of working proved helpful. Once dancers have been given clear direction – or a meaningful piece of music – they throw themselves right into a situation. Without asking questions they jump in at the deep end and find their emotion, and only then do they look, assess and question. By then they've broken the ice and opened up a character's heart and somehow it is easier to build from that position than an intellectual one. What dancers generally don't have is a rich, fluid interesting voice in which to deliver their findings – most dancers' voices are high and without range. However, my voice was not totally hopeless thanks to my Cone Ripman acting classes but I would really have to exercise and work my vocal cords to make my voice strong and true enough for the play.

For the first two days I kept very quiet, watching and listening as the director started blocking the scenes. My role was quite large and all the actors, knowing this was my first professional acting job and that I too had lost my own mother, were kind and generous to me. My timorousness soon disappeared and I threw myself – helped by one and all – into Scrap. After a while I sensed I could do it. The personal experience I could draw on and the fact that I looked exactly like the 'small, thin, rather peaky with a very shy manner' character Miss Smith described helped me enormously. This was my entry into the world of a proper adult theatre company. Here I was, on my own, feeling I was part of a serious theatre and accepted as an actress. I was suddenly aware of a freer world than I was used to – I saw the flirting, the gossip and the affairs-away-from-home that were part of backstage life – but was also buoyed up by the colossal warmth, kindness and mad humour of it all. I felt I would be able to take care of Daddy much better after this experience, that I was becoming a knowledge-able woman of the world who understood a lot more about the needs and emotions of grown-ups.

Every day without fail I got to the theatre early to do my warm-up and barre work, usually hanging on to rickety bits of scenery for support. I daren't let it slip and besides, acting or not, I wanted to practise. Miss Harris, my drama teacher, came from Loddington to see how I was getting along and seemed pleased.

The first performance of the play in front of an audience taught me a lot about the 'enchanted state' that I subsequently always tried to reach before going on in a big role. With Scrap I tried to let her mind and heart overtake mine so that by the time I got on stage I *was* her. Sadly this was very possible, given how recently Mummy had died but nonetheless I had to learn the process and attain the mental separation and concentration on the 'now' that this state demanded. I felt pride during the curtain call of our opening night, not only because of the enthusiastic response from the audience but also the kindness of the older members of the cast. They totally accepted me – I had become one of them. The play was very well received and Scrap had some lovely reviews.

Towards the end of the play's run Daddy managed to get away and come up to Leicester. I didn't want him to, as I felt it would churn him up too much. He tried to hide his pain, but I knew it had a profoundly saddening effect on him. I only prayed that my new grown-up awareness would be a comfort to him.

MONDAY, APRIL 14th, 1941

J. Baxter Somerville and Peter Hoar
(for Associated Theatre Seasons Ltd.)
In Association with Community Theatre (Croydon) Ltd.
present

The Regency Players

— in —

"DEAR OCTOPUS"

By DODIE SMITH.

Charles Randolph		SYDNEY RUSSELL
Dora Randolph		JOAN ROGERS
Hilda Randolph		EDWINA DAY
Margery Harvey	their children	BETTY BELLEW
Cynthia Randolph		DIANA MUIRHEAD
Nicholas Randolph		GODFREY HARRISON
Hugh Randolph		JOHN BARRON
Gwen (Flouncy) Harvey		NORENNE THOMAS
	their Grand-children	by courtesy of Gabrielle de Wilden
William (Bill) Harvey		PAT WOODING
Kathleen (Scrap) Kenton		JILL PYRKE
Belle Schlessinger		PEARL DADSWELL
Edna Randolph (Hugh's Mother)		LUCY GRIFFITHS
Laurel Randolph (Hugh's Wife)		RONA LAURIE
Kenneth Harvey (Margery's Husband)		FRANCIS ROBERTS
Grace Fenning (Dora's Companion)		MARGARET COOPER
Nanny Patching (a Nurse)		JENNIE DILLON
Gertrude a Parlourmaid)		NORA ENTON

PRODUCED BY GODFREY HARRISON

At the end of the run of *Dear Octopus* my chaperone returned to take me back to Loddington and I waved goodbye to all my new-found theatre friends. Soon I was engrossed in school life once more – and things had moved on apace. Sonia and Claudie had both been dancing with small companies that were struggling to ride the impossibilities of the war. They explained how these companies had had no orchestra as all their musicians were in the Armed Forces, but then talented pianists started saving the day by taking the place of whole orchestras. Maggie had leapt ahead in class and was beautiful to watch – she was already an outstanding performer. New games and clubs had been forming; I quickly became a member of one where you had to endure 'torture' to reach the upper echelons. The torture was being held down while your feet were tickled for five minutes – with no screaming. I also returned just in time for our school doctor's monthly check-up. I had grown even thinner as the work in the repertory company had been quite arduous. The doctor examined me and pronounced, 'This child is starving and she must be given milk with Horlicks every night.' So he wrote a prescription for the extra rations of milk that invalids were allowed and which I greedily cherished. This did not go down that well with the other girls.

Soon the fervour of exams took over the school. In 1941 the Royal Academy of Dancing's Solo Seal exam consisted of class work, a solo set by the examiners and a solo to be choreographed by the entrant. Ten of us had been entered for this exam – the ones our teachers believed could achieve the required syllabus and who had already demonstrated interpretative talents. These would have shown up in our repertoire classes and also in the long *enchaînements* – the chain of steps that allow dancers to move across a stage – that teachers sometimes elected to give us at the end of daily class and which meant, after the harsh correctness of the compulsory techniques, you could suddenly let rip and fly.

All ten of us were excited and honoured, and I felt that I had to pull something significant out of the bag so that I did not let the school down. This was daunting, but the Solo Seal was held in high esteem so I knew it was also a colossal springboard and it felt totally invigorating – maybe the Horlicks was helping.

I suppose I should have realised at the time that I was on the verge of taking an important step that would influence my life to come. But as it was I was just a fifteen-year-old revelling in the intriguing process of choreographing, which made me feel whole and real. I didn't for a moment sense it would become the craft that would enable me to work all over the world to this day.

All the exam entrants had their noses thrust deep into books or negotiated extra time in the music room as they searched for subjects for their respective solos. I loved the music room. There were two pianos, a black grand and a dark-brown upright along with a couple of gramophones, stacks of 78 rpm records, books and scores. We became sleuths slinking around the corridors, not wanting to divulge an idea once we'd had it. I had read about the eighteen-year-old Victoria receiving the news in Kensington Palace that she had become Queen and the more I thought about it, the more I could see what I could do with it as a dance subject. I was experiencing a miniature version of what it means and takes to be a choreographer. For this exam my task was to find a story that would engage, match it to music that would not only deliver the story but enhance it, and devise my steps. So, decision made, I set out to find the music that would help me to deliver the scene dramatically as well as choreographically. In the music room I listened to everything that seemed even vaguely suitable.

The musical research for the Solo Seal was making me aware of something I'd taken for granted: the fact that music was central to and totally part of – and necessary to – me. I was beginning to understand that for me, music can be and sometimes is the centre, the meaning, even the reason for life – it's like some wonderful yet almost fearful power, which can move me to almost any emotion. And of course, without music there is no dance – or in any case not dance as I knew it. I had become so immersed that I felt I was only my real self when I was dancing or in the theatre or with my music – all the rest of the time I was or felt like a shadow, a restless shadow wandering aimlessly waiting for life to be breathed into it to give it a real form.

Eventually, I found and chose one of Edward Elgar's *Enigma Variations*, 'Nimrod', and set about creating an acting dance with a base of classical technique, which is what, I suppose, I have tried to do in all my work ever since, although this is by no means the only way of doing it. The process of creating a ballet can start with either music or story (or a painting or a landscape, if it comes to it), the choreographer finding inspiration wherever and however it comes and arranging the other elements accordingly.

For the first time I had to find a way of fitting the plot of my dance – Victoria's life-defining moment – to my chosen music. It was such a satisfying process, allowing my mind's decisions to send my body off on its own journeys, discovering ways of moving to match where my music and mind had gone. It didn't seem to be about finding steps as such, but ways for my body to discover its own delightful and enlightening possibilities. The process of 'telling the story' in dance so that each movement has a clear truth behind it was exciting and rewarding. Truly it was – and is – enthralling.

And then the day came. We all went down to London, stayed overnight and showed up at the RAD on Holland Park Avenue – a place of happiness and deep sorrow for me as it was so closely associated with Mummy and our twice-weekly trips up for my scholarship classes. In front of an audience and a panel of intuitive and discerning examiners we all went through our Solo Seal pieces. When it came to me, I stepped into the upstage right position, stayed still and thought myself into the eighteen-year-old Princess's mind. I looked at my pianist for a fleeting second and off we went.

I started with the youth of the girl and her light-hearted way of dancing through her day and the moment when her maid informed her that the archbishop and Lord Conyngham were asking to see her. Then came the dismissal of her maid and the way the overwhelming news began to swirl around her as she realised her life was about to change, and the tiny moment of panic that induced. She had to compose herself enough to present a serious and worthy persona to the powerful men coming towards her. All of this – her way of life, the room, the sound – transformed into a shattering, shimmering, awe-inspiring moment as she looked down on the heads of the two men genuflecting before her as they acknowledged that she was now the Queen of all things and lands British. Getting her body to accept her inevitable fate as the men led her out and presented her to her nation and the sheer glory of it was something I revelled in, propelled by Elgar's ravishing music. As I finished I felt nervous but exhilarated. The examiners nodded their dismissal of me without a word.

We returned to Loddington and our wise teachers had arranged a performance of our solos for the rest of the school, to stave off the anticlimax and ease the wait for our results. It was very rewarding to be given a second chance at the dance, without the nerves and agitation of the exam. When I finished there was a second's silence and then a joyous burst of applause. I knew my Elgar dance had worked because many of my teachers were in tears at the end. And it had done the trick at the RAD, too – I passed.

FIVE

The Ballet Guild

1941–1943

Looking to the future

IN 1941 THE WAR SAW our country sustain blow after blow and the outcome looked increasingly uncertain. Anxious parents were constantly checking in to see if the school was still functioning at all, let alone well. But there it was, stuck in the Leicestershire countryside with fifty-one unusual, artistic, highly strung teenagers, committed to training them for a life in ballet or musical theatre with all the disciplines that demanded, and trying to keep some kind of balance between that life and the dire global disasters shaking the world outside. Nothing was conventional, nothing was sane, huge adjustments to normal life were required daily and yet, here we were, on the barre, stretching and honing our arabesques, fighting for an extra pirouette or higher jump or deeper split.

The principals decided to arrange two days of show classes . – a selection of pieces and techniques chosen to demonstrate skills and range – in London to remind people of the school's existence and success. The Solo Seal concert at the school had gone well, they were proud of their pupils and they did not want their work to be lost to the theatre world while we were all beavering away so assiduously in the wilds of Leicestershire. Besides, the bombing had become more random and widespread so staying put could be just as risky as being in London. The classes they devised were clever and detailed and minutely prepared. They contained legitimate technical sections of our training but our principals made sure they were entertaining as well. At the end of each class several pupils would perform solos and duets to show off our theatricality. After a lot of competition Maggie, John, Jean, Diana, Brenda and I were among the lucky ones selected. Some very important names in the ballet world were invited to watch.

We all went down to London on the train at night, unable to see the damage in the dark as we neared St Pancras, and were put up at a small hotel near the London school so Matron could keep us all together and under control. Early next morning Miss Knight gave us a long warm-up class at the school and then, still in our practice clothes, we were taken by bus to the Toynbee Hall Theatre on Commercial Street in the East End for our performances.

Hustled in through the stage door we changed into our fresh tunics, socks and tights. We could hear the babble of voices increasing as the hall filled up. Misses Cone and Ripman had gathered an impressive throng including Marie Rambert, the great teacher and artistic director of the Ballet Rambert, who often hired the young choreographer Frederick Ashton; Mona Inglesby, who against all the odds was bravely managing to keep a small London-based ballet company going; and, most important as it turned out for me, Molly Lake. Molly had danced in Anna Pavlova's company alongside the famous ballerina and was herself a strong dancer. She was also the inspired teacher and artistic director of a small company called the Ballet Guild. Finally, Peggy van Praagh, who was an outstanding dancer and an even better teacher, was there.

We were absolutely on our mettle, nervous but excited, frightened but filled with the extra adrenaline our bodies so thoughtfully manufacture for such electric moments. The audience was generous and very interested in us – and you can't ask for anything better than that – so we all did pretty well. I felt myself almost grow into the vibrant atmosphere and found new little surges and balances that I could manage only because of the warmth flooding the stage from our distinguished audience. Afterwards we met and talked to many new people and

I was particularly happy that Molly Lake – with her dark eyes looking intently at me, her authoritative unsentimental voice and matter-of-fact manner – seemed to be paying attention to my work.

The supper our principals had arranged for us after our second performance was a happy, noisy, slightly over-the-top occasion as everyone, young and old, was feeling a bit pleased with themselves. It was a contented and fulfilled little gang of resistance fighters that returned to Loddington the next day. We felt as if we could one day become veterans of the dance world.

Late in 1941 several of us caught an infection, which made us very ill and put us in isolation for a few weeks. We had fevers and no energy, and everyone was worried it was cholera. (Not surprisingly, the bombing Hitler meted out to the Midlands, and the non-stop raids on the whole industrial heart of England, did hit the occasional plumbing and water supply.) After ten days in bed we were allowed to get up for a few hours daily and gradually we returned to health. I had thought the enforced rest might kill me, I found it so difficult to take it easy, but eventually we were allowed out of the isolation area and by then it was nearly Christmas, so most of the girls were sent home anyway. But for a few of us this was not possible – some families, like mine, were splintered because of the war.

Daddy was unable to get leave and besides our own small

Card to thank my father and the RAF, 1941

house was still closed up. Auntie Bess and Uncle Phil could not really cope with a convalescent child, especially as Bess had become chief cashier of the Midland Bank on Croydon High Street and was very busy with work. So everyone agreed it would be better for me to stay at Loddington and gain strength. Five of us remained in the huge house, reading and writing cards by the fires, and listening to music whenever we could. Finally we were allowed to venture outside – wrapped up and looking like unloved penguins.

The New Year, when school had resumed and our friends had returned, brought good news. I was to be sent to London to work with Molly Lake! She needed a classically competent youngster to join her company in London and elsewhere. My school had suggested I would be a suitable choice and she agreed, so the die was cast: I would be at the Ballet Guild when needed and at Loddington in between.

The Ballet Guild was Molly's and her dancer-husband Travis Kemp's creation. Molly was such an outstanding teacher that a great many of the best dancers in the country wanted to work with her. She and Travis had created their boutique company based on this fact; they knew they could tempt many of these stand-out dancers to appear with them for special Sunday performances, galas and charity concerts usually as part of the war effort. As well as the Ballet Guild's own dancers, dancers working full time in other companies could come to Molly's for classes and also these out-of-hours performances, timed so as not to clash with the normal working life of a ballet dancer. It was an unusual set-up. Conventional ballet companies operated quite differently, keeping their dancers busy with a relentless programme of practice classes and rehearsals followed by seasons of performances in their 'home' theatre and then usually one or two periods of touring, or repertory, a year. But, during these war years companies and dancers did what they could to survive.

I was lucky to be able to work with such stellar dancers so young. I learnt so much from them, especially about preparation, conservation, projection and etiquette. It was a crash course in being professional and though the company was small it was impeccable in its balletic standards. I first appeared with them during May 1942, in a series of performances in aid of the Five Arts Gift Fund for Comforts for the Red Army. After a very short rehearsal period I danced a lovely role as one of the 'leading Wilis' – there are two of them – in *Giselle*. It was a little bewildering, totally thrilling artistically and quite shocking because of the danger of being in London. I returned to school even more determined to study hard and talked for hours to Miss Knight, and anyone else who would listen, about how I could improve after my little taste of life in a real ballet company.

Molly Lake

What a start it had been! And I must have risen to the occasion because from then on Molly took a real interest in me. Next she asked me to learn 'Papillon', a solo from Fokine's ballet *Carnaval* – a fiendishly difficult little dance, especially for an inexperienced sixteen-year-old. I was sent to London from Loddington to learn the solo from Molly herself at her studio in St John's Wood.

The studio was near to what I imagined heaven might be like. It had a hardy, old, well-sprung wooden floor, tall dark beams rising up to a high pointed ceiling, elevated windows down one side, great long barres down each side and behind them stood lovely old mirrors, some a little cracked. An area at the end housed a toilet; changing rooms (one male, one female); a little kitchen station with a kettle and mugs; a few armchairs covered with exotic rugs from all over the world, including some from Molly's and Travis's tours with Pavlova; a long bench; a rosin box; an old black piano with music stacked on top and toppling off it; and a slightly mysterious winding staircase leading up to a gallery overlooking the studio, which was Molly's domain. It was the dream environment for a dancer to work in. There was a constant stream of dancers – young, middle-aged, famous, unheard-of, dark and thrilling, pale and fascinating, extrovert or shy – passing through. Every single one loved that studio, worshipped Molly as a tough, inspiring teacher and wanted desperately to work with her.

As the newest – and, at just sixteen, marginally the youngest – recruit I was kindly treated but nonetheless I was expected to fall in at rehearsals with eagerness and intelligence. As well as concentrating on what was going on in front of me I also had to field the whispered advice that came from the excellent dancers behind me – Gerd Larsen, David Paltenghi and Peggy van Praagh – which made me feel proud but also a little anxious at the same time. Gerd was always helpfully correcting me in a no-nonsense way, while David was gentler and imaginative in his advice. He was drop-dead gorgeous and elegant so anything he had to say, good or bad, was thrilling. Peggy, who I knew was watching me closely, never missed overseeing my attempts at *piqué* turns across the room, or my *fouettés* and jumps.

One day I was to be coached by Molly on my own for the first time. It was just her, the pianist and me. She started by saying, '"Papillon" – the butterfly – has lightning speed, fast changes of direction and pirouettes that skim with no weight in them. These are the qualities we must have in this dance.' She proceeded to show me the fiendish steps move by move. She had a way of willing you to do it and we took it phrase by phrase, not moving on until I had understood all aspects of each – even if I was still wavering. Molly was very tall for a dancer and her intensity as she watched me – correcting each attempt until my body had taken it in, her willpower hovering over us so that there was nothing else but the dance in the room – was all-commanding. I *had* to do it – and so I did. I felt like a clumsy oaf at first, but her obvious desire for me to deliver this dance was incredibly helpful. After an hour and a half of intense concentration she pronounced, 'Enough, Jill. Enough. You have understood it, the speed will come, you are just stumbling through it now but it will be very good. I am pleased. So change now, go back to school and *practise*! We'll get you to perform it soon.'

I certainly practised and when, only a couple of weeks later, the Ballet Guild was part of a Sunday concert in aid of the war effort at the diminutive Arts Theatre in central London I was ready to present my 'Papillon' solo. To be part of a truly professional dance performance was incredible. To be in the wings alongside the brilliantly witty dancer Beryl Kaye – funny, scathing, dry and warm all at the same time – Pauline Clayden, who was like a real-life Ariel; David, the heart flutterer; Gerd, who was grand and stunning; Peggy, so powerful and mature; and indeed Molly and Travis, who were all so much older and more sophisticated and experienced made my spine grow at least two inches. To watch at the end how they took their calls so radiantly (even though I knew how tired most of them were, as they were also dancing full time with other companies), to be pushed on for the finale sometimes only having learnt it five minutes before the show, the whole business of *being in the ballet* in a small packed-out theatre in wartime so everyone's nerves and emotions – performers and audience – were heightened, it was like being rocketed to another planet. My eyes were popping out of my head. There was so much to see, learn and do, and I was very glad to be embraced by this happy band of dancers. I was near bursting point. I seemed to have leapt over a bubbling stream and landed on the bank of a new and undiscovered country.

Molly, having trained and danced with Pavlova, seemed to think she had found something of the 'Russian spirit' in me. She began teaching me Fanchon Fadette, the lead role in her own ballet, *La Petite Fadette*, which she had based on the George Sand novel before commissioning a lovely score by Gabriel Fauré, in order to see if her hunch was correct. Did I indeed seem to have the technique and acting ability she could build into a young lead for her company?

When Molly didn't need me I would go back to Loddington Hall. One of my teachers would come and fetch me and would always try to stay and watch if Molly was coaching me. This was nerve-racking but it also made me feel excited. Back at school they re-enforced the training, especially my most inspirational teacher Marian Knight, who was delighted at these chances her pupil was being given. Eventually, however, it became clear that if I was to give myself fully to being a part of Ballet Guild, it would be sensible to leave Loddington for good. Molly was beginning to need me more and more for rehearsals, and it was obvious I was on the threshold of joining her company full time and that she was wanting to train me up to become a soloist. It was a turning point.

It wasn't an easy decision. I was happy at school. The long walks in the country, the games, the tadpoling, the late-night talks trying to understand all that was going on in the war, the occasional feasts when someone's mother had sent a food parcel up to Loddington, were all great fun to be part of. Maggie had become like a sister to me, I was very close to John Gilpin and all the Solo Seal entrants, Marian Knight and Betty Davis had become advisers as well as teachers and I felt very fond of them: Loddington had become my home. So Daddy and Auntie Bess thrashed it out with Molly *and* the dear women at school and after a lot of to-ing and fro-ing my fate was decided. There was another sixteen-year-old girl in the corps de ballet whose parents had a house near Molly's headquarters in Loudon Road. Mr and Mrs Garner indicated that I could stay with them declaring, 'It is as easy to look after two dancers as it is one.'

Slightly reluctantly and very tearfully, therefore, at the end of 1942 I left Loddington and my schooldays – and any hope of an academic education – for good.

Everything looked and felt highly promising, but I was about to get a shock. The Garners were welcoming, the house was bright and light, with everything painted pale cream, and the room I was to share with Mary was comfortable with a lovely armchair – and a double bed. Somehow I thought I'd have my own bed. I quickly chastised myself about this and remembered all the unlikely and uncomfortable places my fellow students and I had been forced to sleep in over the past few years. Anyway, everything went well for the first week. Mary and I walked the few minutes to Molly's studio each day and it was great to be able to work flat out in class without having had a long journey to get there. Mrs Garner always had soup or something nice for us when we got home, full of chatter and notes to compare about the day's rehearsals. Then one night, when we had been in bed for a couple of hours, I awoke to the feeling of having my breast stroked. Mary was whispering in my ear, 'You're such a little thing.'

She was right: I had no breasts at all that you could actually see, but that didn't give her the right to touch them. Even though we were same age it seemed we were at quite different stages. I got hold of her hand and pushed it away, but she continued, 'Jill, don't be frightened. There's nothing wrong in this and you need a lot of love!'

By now I was lying there like an electrified twig after a storm. It wasn't in me to be rude, she and her family were being so generous, and Mary was a perfectly lovely girl. Had she been a boy the shock would have been less extreme but, as it stood, I didn't want Mary to touch my breasts or anything else. I felt completely trapped but managed to mumble, 'Don't do that, and please don't be upset.'

I turned over and tried to sleep. The next day I was tired and taut, and couldn't help thrashing the whole thing over in my head as I tried to get through my rehearsals without mishap. Molly didn't say anything but noticed and observed everything. The following night when we were in bed I asked Mary not to touch me and for an hour she did not. I was sleeping badly when suddenly she became very amorous in spite of my trying to talk her out of it with 'It's not that I don't think you are nice and even lovely looking. It is just that I have a goal in my life about being pure until I marry and this isn't part of that goal, so please stop!' I got up, put a sweater over my nightdress and slept on the floor.

The next day I crept out of the house early, went to the post office and rang my Auntie Bess. I just caught her as she was leaving for the bank and asked if I could please come back to Addiscombe Road. Sounding extremely anxious, she asked me why. I stammered, 'Well . . . I can't seem to get along properly with Mary and it is . . . um . . . well, anyway, I can't sleep and I'm so unhappy about it. They have been so kind but please, Auntie, I've got to come home!'

She finally said, 'I'll ask your uncle to come and meet you off the 5.30 train from Victoria and we'll talk all about it then.'

It was hard telling the Garners that I had to go back to East Croydon but I couldn't land Mary in it. So they never knew why I left and when I told Auntie Bess that night I tried to be as woolly as possible to protect Mary from what would have been my aunt's fury. I was slightly worried about how things would be in class with Mary but decided we would both be so busy it should be relatively easy to avoid the issue.

So it was back to the daily trek from East Croydon to London to work with Molly, typically getting up at 7 a.m. and squeezing into the bathroom early before my aunt and uncle. I would pack my practice bag, dash carefully down the narrow, steep stairs, turn on the radio, put on the kettle and lay the dining table so that we could all have tea and bread with margarine and marmalade (Grandma Hart had managed to make some early in the war) together. Often we discussed the news on the radio. We were terribly excited about the emergence of 'Monty' – General Bernard Montgomery. Then I'd rush for the bus with Auntie who was going on to Croydon and the bank. I leapt off at East Croydon station and waited to board the train to Victoria as it chugged in. I would climb aboard, find a seat if possible or a place to lean, and listen intently to the animated chat between businessmen and workers of all shapes and sizes, with a smattering of uniformed men and women. Words like Tripoli, Monty and the desert flew through the air even though everyone was aware that 'careless talk costs lives'. I tried to glean what I could so I could sound a little more in the know at Molly's – or at least not totally ignorant. Then I'd push down the platform at Victoria and on to the No. 82 bus to St John's Wood, run the last five minutes to Molly's studio on Loudon Road and change my clothes as fast as possible so as to get a good place on the barre.

The chord to announce 'first positions' would quieten the hubbub of dancers' prattle and class would be under way. Barre work, pirouettes at the barre, stretches on the barre, centre work, *adage*, adagio, fast *battements*, *petits battements*, *brisés*, smooth flowing *enchaînements*, *sautés*, *fouettés*, big steps to work on elevation, pirouettes of all kinds, sharp point work, *manèges*, *révérence* and finish – an hour and a half later. You would either be elated because you'd sealed an improvement or depressed because you could not correct an ongoing fault (in my case my overarched back coupled with 'shoulders-up' was a sign of too much tension). We stretched out on the floor or lay flat with our bottoms against the skirting board, legs stretched vertically up the wall, or relaxed in *seconde* on the floor with legs stretched wide to the side, body resting on the floor in between. Molly would be clapping her hands and we would all jump up as she announced the day's rehearsals and any news. Then it was straight to work on a ballet.

I had a lot of work to do as I was new and Molly wanted to get me into most of the ballets to be presented in March at the Garrick Theatre – *Chartres*, *Les Sylphides*, *Grand Divertissement*, *Swan Lake* and *La Petite Fadette*. We would break for an hour and a quarter for lunch. Nearly everyone would bring packets of biscuits, carrots, a couple of apples or a marmite sandwich or there was a café near Swiss Cottage. Often, as she observed I hardly brought anything with me – no time for that at Addiscombe Road in the early morning – Molly would take me across the road to her and Travis's lovely old house and give me a bowl of soup and talk to me about the history of dance, the war or the ballets we were rehearsing.

Then it was back to rehearsal and often – best of all – new

choreography. It was tremendously exciting to be part of the writing of a ballet, the development of the story to be told through dance, the creation of the steps, understanding how it should relate to an eventual score, and there was much laughter as we attempted things we couldn't accomplish yet, fell over a lot or were saved at the last minute from hitting the deck by one of the men. There was endless gossip and I learnt all there was to know about the dancer's 'moan'. All dancers hurt from early on in their lives because every day they ask too much of their bodies. The body starts to say, 'Hey wait a minute! I don't want to do that,' only to be told, 'Well, you are going to, so come on, try harder. Get on with it. Give me that extra stretch (or strength or spring) I asked for!' Hence in the end, when it all gets too much, the body and the brain finally collude and out comes a remonstrance known as 'the moan'. Everyone indulges in it, with good reason, and though I did not hurt yet I knew it would only be a matter of time.

Usually I was allowed to leave at 5 p.m. because I had the journey back to East Croydon, but I always went reluctantly. I vastly enjoyed life in that studio! I would walk to and wait for the bus, sit and go through what I'd learnt in my mind, become part of the moving populace on the concourse of Victoria, join the train – chug-chug – back to East Croydon, with luck not having to wait too long for the bus at the other end, but sometimes I was so elated I would just set straight off from the station and leg it back. At home we would all be tired but buoyed up by sharing tales of the day, there would be news on the radio to digest, supper to eat, nothing exciting food-wise thanks to our rationing, and then we would crash into bed. Once in a while a jazz pianist friend of my aunt's would appear and lift us all with his off-beat rhythms and sensual sounds. I would dance around the small living room and on those nights would enjoy a happy, relaxed sleep.

My professional life really began with wartime performances in places like the Garrick Theatre in aid of causes such as the Women's Junior Air Corps (Holborn Unit No. 162). In early 1943 the programme was devised for a week of eight performances in Wolverhampton at the Wulfen Hall organised under a contract with the Entertainment National Service Association – ENSA. Since very early on in the war the Ballet Guild had been part of this ENSA effort and had been giving performances throughout England as a result. The shows would usually consist of a series of single acts extracted from famous ballets, usually lasting about two hours, and would be repeated about four times over two or three days before we'd move on to the next place. Sometimes these events were one-offs, sometimes they were real tours lasting several weeks. I was finally to dance Fanchon Fadette in Molly's *La Petite Fadette* in public for the first time. I was also now to dance under the name of Gillian, as Molly felt Jill was too plain and simple for the stage.

WULFRUN HALL
WOLVERHAMPTON

Week beginning Monday, 3rd May, 1943
Nightly at 6.30

Matinee Wednesday, Thursday and Saturday
at 2.30

The Ballet Guild

UNDER THE DIRECTION OF
DERYCK LYNHAM

Maître de Ballet - - - - - MOLLY LAKE
Assistant Maître de Ballet ANNA SEVERSKAYA
Stage Manager - - - PETER HAMLYN
GERD LARSEN, GILLIAN PYRKE
TRAVIS KEMP, HANK VAN DER BRINK
ALEX THOMSON, ELIZABETH ALLISON
ANNA SEVERSKAYA, PETER HAMLYN
BALLET GUILD QUINTET
Leader: NEVILLE MARRINER Pianist: MAVIS BARR

All Seats Bookable - - 2/- 3/- 4/-
Booking Days and Tickets at the Civic Hall Box Office
Telephone 22456

At the start of the war Wolverhampton had been listed as a German bombing target, along with Birmingham and Coventry, particularly because the skilled labour force helped manufacture aircraft, tyres, ammunition and carburettors for Spitfires and Lancasters. Bomb raids had devastated parts of the city in 1942 but as we left Euston Station the news was quite different – the billboards were all about the German surrender in Russia.

When I arrived at the theatre Gerd Larsen greeted me with a hug and said, 'Shall we go up to the foyer and run through the opening of *La Petite*?' As always, Gerd looked very beautiful. She had high cheekbones, beautiful skin and blonde hair, and was wearing a very glamorous coat, which I'd gladly have dragged off her back in exchange for my old school navy one. From the start she was very bossy, yet also very positive and very caring towards me. Gerd was much in demand as a solo performer and danced with many companies, but she always tried to make her classes with Molly, in whom she believed intrinsically. She was dancing Odette, the Swan Princess, in Act Two of *Swan Lake* during our Wolverhampton stint, but as she knew I was dancing Fadette – the changeling – for the first time, she thoughtfully suggested we mark it through while Molly and Travis coped with the lighting. So off we went to the empty foyer to go through the opening several times, humming the Fauré score, so I could really feel relaxed from the start.

The 'get-in' to a new theatre is usually touch and go. To hang the cloths, see the lights focused and their plot registered, to 'place' the ballets on the new stage, to run through each ballet with the musicians (Molly's artistic and persuasive powers had gathered an excellent quintet to play for her company, where most struggling companies had only a pianist), for the wardrobe to unpack and iron the costumes, then get each to the correct dressing room in the two hours before 'the half' (the thirty-five minutes before curtain up) is a tall order, and one little setback can throw the precarious balance off. So, I didn't ask if I could have a run-through, not even of my *pas de deux* with Travis, the first I had ever done, since I knew it would throw everything out. This was to be my first attempt at a leading role. I was nervous but not frightened, and I wasn't alone – absolutely everyone felt the same and that helped. And I was particularly lucky to have Travis as my partner, with his kindness, experience and strength.

With Travis Kemp in La Petite Fadette, *1943*

I *think* our show went well. I was in such a mixed state of euphoria – I had been trusted to play the female lead in a ballet I loved, and then there was the sheer thrill of a first night as a regular member of the Ballet Guild, plus the effervescence needed for Molly's *Victorian Bouquet* in which the whole company had to fizz and sparkle like champagne – that I'm not sure I could ever have given an accurate, critical assessment of the evening. But I do know I was happy to be part of such a vibrant group of performers and that I went home to our digs and slept with ease.

The next morning we were to be 'called' at 11.30 for class, so some of us went out for a walk to see how damaged the little workhorse of a town had become. Wolverhampton was grey-mauve with scars of brown-orange slashed across it. Everyone in England by now was used to the angular piles of broken beams and brick punctuating what had been neat, purposeful little streets, all their cruel injuries gathered together and tidied up so that people could continue their journeys to work, the damage to their lives contained. The whole of the English workforce – those left at home to bolster the war effort to feed our Army's, Air Force's and Navy's needs – knew they had to absorb their wounds, and the shock and hurt, and soldier on with life with as much energy and will as they could muster. That night I gave a much better performance because of feeling part of that town: a performance not just based on a selfish ambition to shine, but a desire to give something to the people who, in the midst of all the problems inflicted by war, had felt moved to come out and buy a ticket to the ballet. This appreciation lodged firmly in my heart, to be carefully retained ever since. The week went well. Not even the Mary Garner situation got in the way – there's nothing like pulverising performances and rehearsals to knock anything as silly as resentment out of the window. I found dancing with Travis a joy, Gerd was beautiful as Odette . . . and all too soon we were on our way back to London.

Some relief from the horrors of war came in the form of Monty's triumph and Rommel's defeat. The surrender of the

Axis Forces in North Africa gave England a huge lift. Suddenly, people were smiling and they even started to look different. Fabric rationing had scuppered any hope of real sartorial splendour but, even so, the ingenuity people had discovered in making new clothes out of old, raiding long forgotten trunks in the attics and adapting all manner of unlikely materials in an attempt to conjure fashion out of very little was nothing short of miraculous. The full effect of these efforts seemed to have reached a pitch in early 1943. Men wore suits and hats. If women could lay their hands on nylons they had seams down the back and if they could not find nylons they drew a line down the backs of their legs to simulate them. Women wore suits too, not skin tight but straight and neat, and the mingling of civvy and Forces suits had the effect of making London look smart and alert to fashion even though it was made from very little. This didn't apply to me, of course. I spent all my time in a little jersey dress – with striped top and plain bottom – and in any case most days were taken up with practice clothes: tights, pants and cross-over tops. When it was cold I had my trusty plain navy school coat, which went over everything.

I was saved from looking like a complete urchin by Ed Turner, whose wife had been driving the car that terrible day in Coventry. He had kept in touch with Daddy and me, and was fully aware that I was finding it tough without a mother. He was very important by now and had recently designed a generator for the Air Ministry using a Triumph vertical twin engine. He came to London for two days on business but let Daddy know in advance and said he'd like to take me shopping. I was delighted to see him. We may have been linked by sorrow but he was also a great novelty – very chic, very smart, very rich and very nice. He was completely different from the world I had become part of and was therefore utterly captivating. Molly let me off afternoon rehearsals and Ed came to pick me up at the studio to take me for lunch. I introduced them and realised that 'the ballet' was as intriguing to him as his world was to me. Off we went to Fortnum & Mason in Piccadilly. This was hallowed ground: the rich man's grocers, it was smart, beautiful and somehow, even then, packed with fine food and lovely clothes. We had a lunch the like of which I had not eaten since one of Mummy's de luxe picnics in the bluebells; we talked incessantly and then we visited the upstairs clothes department and found long socks, two little skirts, two beautiful woollen jumpers to match them and a dear little camel hair coat with a braided collar to round it all off. We were on our way out, with me in another world by now and all but tearful at my good fortune, when Ed said, 'Shoes, Jill, we must have a pair of shoes to bind it all together!'

And back we went to find the shoe department, where we discovered a perfect pair of patent lace-ups. The joy of it was that I was aware that the experience had been just as happy and fulfilling for Ed, and we were somehow joined for ever knowing full well that each of us wished – oh, how strongly we wished – that we'd had two other dear, dear people with us. It was with deep sadness and true gratitude that I said goodbye to him that day.

The next morning I arrived at class with my head held high, rather proud of my new look. No sooner had I entered the studio than Molly leaned over her balcony, saying, 'Jill, I would like to see you up here for a minute.'

I mounted the stairs to her holy of holies, whereupon she made four pronouncements. The first was, 'The reaction to your work in Wolverhampton was excellent. Really excellent!'

I tried not to show how pleased I was while she continued, 'But the comment about your name was not favourable. It is too easy to misspell, as you'll see from the notices pinned on the board downstairs. Because of that, I think it does you a disservice. I am sure you will have a long career but it will not be as Gillian Pyrke. Your new name needs to be strong, maybe something very English like mine, and I need to change it to something else because' – and she paused for very dramatic effect – 'I want you to dance Odette in the second act of *Swan Lake* for a special gala evening in August and we cannot have Gillian Pyrke as the Swan Princess. The final thing I want to say to you is you need a holiday. Let's find out from your father if you could holiday near to where he is stationed. All right, darling? Off you go and change for class.'

The sun burst forth as I slid down the stairs from her eyrie. I was one super-happy – but nervous – dancer.

SIX

Baby Ballerina

1943–1944

Swan Lake

INDING MY FATHER'S EXACT WHEREABOUTS wasn't easy. Everything about the defence of aerodromes was hush-hush. When Major Leslie Pyrke was finally located he was busy preparing Ford and Tangmere aerodromes to become the air-sea rescue headquarters for the south coast and Channel. The Battle of the Atlantic was raging and our losses were devastating, so new techniques for picking up airmen and seamen – shot down, half-drowned, injured and trying to keep afloat and save themselves – were being developed and improved daily. Having looked after Croydon during the

Battle of Britain, Daddy was experienced in organising the infrastructure for recovery, subsequent medical help and the transport required beyond that: these problems were safe in his hands.

Until his house near Ford aerodrome was ready, he was staying at the Norfolk Arms in Arundel. He answered the telephone with, 'Yes, who is it?'

'Daddy, it's me! Oh, I've so much to tell you and I only wish you can do it.'

'Do what, darling?' said a slightly bemused father.

'Well, the most exciting thing has happened. Molly wants me to dance Odette, the Swan Princess, in a special celebration show at the People's Palace. She's got to change my name, no one gets ours right. Everything went well with *Fadette* in Wolverhampton and that's why I've got Odette, but she says I must have a holiday, so I want to come down and be with you. Is that possible?'

This must have been the last thing Daddy needed at such a time. He set about patiently trying to unravel my garbled overexcited words and came face to face with reality: a holiday was necessary and he was the obvious choice. I needed him both emotionally and practically. Suddenly, it was all magically arranged. Auntie Bess helped me pack a small case and put me on the train to Brighton where a junior NCO from headquarters whisked me to the Norfolk Arms. Arundel has an omnipresent castle overhanging the tightly packed town, at the centre of which is a steep hill with shops hanging on for dear life down either side. At the bottom of the hill the fast-flowing River Arun hurries across the downs, curtseying to the grandeur of the castle on its right, and past the old Black Rabbit pub before it curves round past the villages of Ford and Climping, finally to meet up with the sea at Littlehampton. The NCO, who was not much older than me, told me to expect my father at approximately 6 p.m. and asked the hotel manager whether he would show Major Pyrke's daughter to her room.

There followed a week of sheer enjoyment. Just to be near Daddy was pure joy anyway, to have the chance to spill out all my news, worries and secret hopes was a relief and a comfort. I was taken to meet my father's staff at both aerodromes and I felt I was nearer the war effort with all its danger and resolve. In contrast, I keenly felt the sea air and my holiday, after six hours of rehearsal a day, was actually helping me to feel fitter and eager to start again. I was also able to observe my father, and for the first time since my mother's death I sensed an inkling – and that's all it was – of the possibility of him coming back to life. This was an advance. I felt he was not totally dead inside and that there was the chance, at some point, of his finding someone else to love him.

I said goodbye to him at the station feeling vibrantly alive, refreshed and full of gratitude for our happy, fulfilled week. I was much reassured about his well-being, knowing that he was at home in his job and enjoying it to the full. I was ready and deter-mined to take on the incredible challenge Molly had offered me.

Fanchon Fadette, Ballet Guild, 1943

When I returned to the studio and looked at the rehearsal sheets and plans for the August shows I was exceedingly glad I had tasted the sea air and had such a relaxed time. We were to start with a week at the Rudolf Steiner Hall in north-west London, before moving on to the Toynbee Hall Theatre in Aldgate East and, finally, a two-week run at the People's Palace in the East End. Seasons in ballet companies can be two or three weeks in length or, like theatre or opera, they can be as long as two or three months. As the Ballet Guild was a small company – and keeping any company going in the war was difficult – this two-week season at the People's Palace was quite a big deal. In 1943 very few expensive, full-length ballets such as the four Acts of *Swan Lake* were able to be mounted by any company, so we usually performed three or four shorter pieces (twenty to thirty minutes in length) and sometimes a *divertissement* as well as a selection of favourite solos and *pas de deux* from the classics.

Starting on 7 August, at the Rudolf Steiner Hall, the matinée programme was to be selections from *Swan Lake*, *The Nymphenburg Garden* – a ballet Molly had choreographed, set to Mozart – as well as her *La Petite Fadette*. I was to dance Odette in the first ballet, an ensemble section and fast duet in the second and the lead in the third. In the evenings my work would include the mazurka from *Les Sylphides*, *Nymphenburg* again, with Molly's *La Valse* and a *Grand Divertissement* to finish. No wonder I'd been sent on holiday. But of course, I was as pleased as Punch and felt the rush of adrenaline that the responsibility of being chosen for special roles gives all theatre people. It's as if all your best talents rush to the surface yelling, 'I'm ready! I'll work! I'll shine – just watch!' and you become twice as strong as you were before.

The studio, which I found such a great place for work,

Ballet Guild, Les Sylphides, *1943*

became even more alive throughout June and July, everyone was very busy – and of course I was busiest of all. The presto duet in *Nymphenburg Garden* was new to me and was a tricky little piece of dance to get under my belt, but it was nothing in comparison with the painstaking way in which Molly and Travis taught me the Swan Princess.

All true classical dance students and junior performers feel they *know* Odette, the Swan Princess in *Swan Lake*. It is the equivalent of Shakespeare's Juliet or the young Prince Hamlet, a role to dream about, to study, to have the confidence to hope that 'one day, I shall be ready to play this role'. However, when you actually come to playing these roles, you often find you know very little and when you delve into what makes those characters come alive it is a revelation. On top of this, I was being coached – ah, what a special word that is! – by two people who had had the privilege of working alongside Pavlova. The whole experience was so illuminating that I ended each rehearsal happy, hurting, determined and daunted. And, in a way perhaps only performers who are totally fulfilled by this process can truly understand, I was also utterly gratified and humbled.

Although I had danced my first *pas de deux* in *Fadette*, the *Swan Lake* pas de deux was in a league of its own. Thanks to Molly's tough training, the technical side of it was already very possible for me. However, learning to touch and nestle into Travis as the Swan Princess, a bird whose inner soul was a woman's, was intriguing and difficult, and creating the swan's neck and arm movements was fascinating but demanding. But Travis was so charming, strong and knowledgeable that these rehearsals were true voyages of discovery – I was also learning how satisfying it can be to dance so closely with a partner you can trust.

Later I would struggle with the *pas de deux*, telling myself there was nothing wrong with enjoying wrapping myself around a man's body – for all *pas de deux* are usually the embodiment of lovemaking – and that I was good at it, all the while hearing my mother insisting, 'Darling, you must try to present a virginal untouched body to a possible husband.' I was about to enter a time of mental struggle over how to stay faithful to my mother's words as I started waking up to the possibilities of sex, but for now there was only the complete ease and pleasure of dancing the *pas de deux* partnered by someone as talented as Travis Kemp. He made me enjoy every aspect, even the little stilted shunts – *terre-à-terre*, or ground-to-ground, hops – released by the beautiful lifts that punctuate every three and a half bars. Between them he and Molly guided me through the role so that I learnt from and loved every minute. I could not have been happier.

I tried really deeply to emulate the swan's glorious neck, to bend my back over as far as I could, with wings quivering below and behind or high up and above depending on the direction of the bend, and to execute the *petite batterie* at the end of the solo still very much as a bird-woman, not some

Swan Lake, *Ballet Guild, 1943*

show-off technician at the end of class. The company was very supportive and I felt it was 'our' performance, not just mine. I was a little saddened by my tutu, though. There was hardly a hint of a feather and it was kept up by a simple hoop – a circle of bone – not endless white frills. Still, I was going out there to earn my status not assume it, so even that was fine.

I was also inspired by the news that my old friend from Miss Sharp's, Beryl Grey, had recently danced her first full-length *Lac des Cygnes* at the age of fifteen – eighteen months younger than I was. Ninette de Valois, the director of the Sadler's Wells Ballet, had deemed she was ready despite her youth. While my mother was alive she had taken me to see ballet at the Sadler's Wells Theatre on Rosebery Avenue when she could afford it. These great occasions always rendered me nigh on impossible to deal with as I became feverishly excited before and after. I saw Alicia Markova, Pearl Argyle, Pamela May, Robert Helpmann and a young Margot Fonteyn in different ballets – *The Haunted Ballroom, Le Roi Nu, Horoscope* and of course the classic *Lac des Cygnes*. Our heated discussions about the dancers and their merits, the marvellous atmosphere at the theatre, which had it seemed been created purely for dance, made the journey along Rosebery Avenue through the West End to Victoria Station and back home to Bromley fly past. There was never any doubt in either of our minds as to where we both hoped my life would lead. The war and Mummy's death had naturally stopped all these exciting visits to Sadler's Wells but they had entrenched an ambition in my heart to be a part of it. I was very pleased for Beryl, perhaps because it fed this hope. It was an extraordinary achievement, but Beryl had always been a star performer, even when I'd first seen her at Madeleine Sharp's, when she was only six.

On the morning of 2 August 1943 I was standing outside the Rudolf Steiner Hall before starting the week's 'get-in' when I looked at the big poster by the entrance and saw a new name on the Ballet Guild programme – Gillian Lynne – and thought instantly that we must have someone new joining us. It was quite a shock when Molly whispered in my ear, 'Don't be silly, Gillian, that's you!' After a while I quite liked the name and anyway I had no choice, for there it was. I only hoped that my father would like it, too.

The week at the Rudolf Steiner and our subsequent performances at the Toynbee Hall Theatre in Aldgate East were
excellent preparation for the run at the People's Palace in the
East End that was to come. I realised that Molly had great
hopes for these big London concerts – especially the forthcoming People's Palace – but had no idea of their real
significance. All through 1943 she had worked tirelessly on the
same group of dancers but she had also been developing and
strengthening her own lead dancer – albeit one now with a
very un-Russian-sounding name.

The People's Palace, Mile End Road, had, after a damaging
fire in the 1930s, been rebuilt to include in its educational
facilities a very large concert hall with a vaulted ceiling and
for our season there I was to be on in every ballet, playing at
least two of the leads and now firmly entrusted with the role
of Odette.

Fuelled by an excess of adrenaline and a new feeling of
privilege I set to work with a will, barely aware of the war and
its tragedies and triumphs, telling Daddy about my progress
when I could reach him by telephone and endlessly grateful to
have such fine teaching to guide me. Travis was so sympathetic
a partner that I became much better at acting Odette's sorrow
and yearning for the Prince's love when we danced together. All
that discipline made the technical side come easier to me, I
enjoyed it completely and without fear, and I could now fill out
the solo properly, since we had already worked so meticulously

to create the swan's arms, back, stamina and speed. We all felt a wave of anticipation gaining strength week after week.

Then suddenly there were only two days to go. The technical 'get-in' to the People's Palace went as smoothly as such detailed comings together of scenery, musicians, wardrobe fittings, stage management's endless checking duties, lighting focusing, performers and directors ever can. Nerves always run high and there is usually, under the studied professional calm and purpose, a beating heart driven by excitement, which charges the air with expectancy and promise – it is thrilling. I was delighted by the size of the auditorium. When I stood in the centre of the stage trying to 'feel the house' – meaning the auditorium – it loomed away into the darkness and drew you in. I had never yet danced in such a large space and this size would really help to lift me up to the last notch I had to attain for these performances.

I had been given a dressing room of my own for the first time and this had a slightly sobering effect on me, which is probably what Molly wanted. Although I missed the girlie dressing-room chat I was used to, it enabled me to think and prepare and realise that I bore a huge responsibility to our company. I *had* to become a ballerina for this little season and being alone helped me to enter that realm, frightening though it was.

On 26 August 1943 the Ballet Guild dedicated their perform-ance to A. V. Coton, the revered ballet critic, and we danced Act Two of *Swan Lake* and sections from two of Molly's popular ballets including *La Petite Fadette*. A. V. Coton was the new London correspondent of the American journal *Dance News*. He was immensely influential as the critic and writer who had helped Antony Tudor form London Ballet in 1938. He was much liked and people paid attention to his pronouncements, so the evening attracted a starry audience.

Through the half-hour leading up to the call of 'beginners please' there had been a steady stream of people coming into my little room to wish me good luck. I was beginning to feel a bit tearful. There's something about a lot of goodwill handed to you with such honest intent that connects straight to my emotional stream and weakens it. I was immensely grateful and amazed by the whole event but, thank goodness, this was stopped abruptly by Molly issuing me with last-minute bang-on-the-nose instructions.

Finally I made my way quietly into the wings, stretched for the last time – legs, back, feet and fingers – scraped my feet in the rosin box and stood in the upstage left wing ready for my entrance. It is a wondrous moment. Standing poised on a very high cliff, committed to a daring high dive must feel similar. You feel you have been chosen by the gods and must summon spiritual forces from God knows where to help launch you from the cliff – you feel special and then your nerves float away as the moment arrives for you to go on.

Odette runs on in the wake of her terrified swans who have circled round the stage and are cowering downstage left at the sight of the alien being – the Prince, and a huntsman at that – and she circles, powerful arms thrashing the air, and comes to a halt in front of her swans, arms flung out to protect them, eyes blazing as she confronts the Prince.

It was a good night, everyone on stage was geed-up by the high-powered audience and, thanks to the weeks of careful coaching, I was able to give my best, at times surprising Molly and even myself. The applause was generous and as we went forward to bow on our own for the third time, Travis hissed in my ear, 'I didn't tell, as I didn't want you to be nervous . . .'

He paused and I said, 'Tell me what, Travis?'

'Look at the centre of the second row. The lady beside Peggy is Ninette de Valois.'

I walked forward for my solo bow and fixed my eye on the second row. I quickly recognised Peggy van Praagh and beside her in black was one of British ballet's finest, Ninette de Valois. I couldn't know it at that moment but, as I gave my best and lowest curtsey, my life changed for ever.

The name de Valois sent shivers down the spine of any aspiring artist hoping to get a chance to work near her company. She had been a member of Ballet Russes in the mid 1920s with Serge Diaghilev, the celebrated impresario. She had 'created' roles – making them entirely her own – in some famous ballets including *Le Train Bleu*, a ballet made for the great English dancer Anton Dolin, and *Les Biches*, with fine and very unusual steps and groups choreographed by Nijinska. She was surrounded by the unique talents in art, dance and music discovered and promoted by Diaghilev – she had learnt from the master himself. When she left Paris and returned to London she established the Academy of Choreographic Arts – a dance school for girls – which immediately attracted the attention of the theatre producer Lilian Baylis, who ran the Old Vic and had campaigned to rebuild the Sadler's Wells Theatre, rescuing it from iniquity, in the 1920s. These two incredibly strong and unusual women had joined the forces of the Sadler's Wells Theatre and the Old Vic, to offer alternating programmes of ballet and opera. Ninette de Valois created the Sadler's Wells Ballet School, and the repertory ballet company the Vic-Wells Ballet, to operate alongside the Vic-Wells Opera Company. In 1939 the whole ballet side became known as the Sadler's Wells Ballet and the opera company became the Sadler's Wells Opera. These were the foundations of two of England's most impressive and lasting theatre dynasties.

Now, 'Madam', as she was universally known, was looking to swell the numbers of her popular ballet company battling to entertain a war-trodden British population, and with so many boys in the Forces she needed her girls to be extra strong in technique. I must have made an impression on her because Madam instantly obtained my address and telephone number and, the following morning, contacted my Auntie Bess. Straight to the point she said, 'I want your niece in my company.'

To my horror Auntie Bess's reply was: 'No, Madam de Valois, that's very good to hear but my niece will not be joining your ballet company, she is too young and besides, she hasn't even had her first period yet!'

When Auntie Bess told me what she had said I could have died of shame and, frankly, couldn't believe the injustice of it. I don't think Auntie could have known how important Ninette de Valois was and that an accolade from her was equivalent to a summons from Terpsichore, the muse of dancing, herself. And of course I found the allusion to my lack of periods at the age of seventeen very embarrassing.

But it cannot have been an easy decision for my aunt. She was having to stand in for both my parents. Perhaps she was just being protective but she may well also have been influenced by Molly Lake's advice that more special training would turn Jill Pyrke, an interesting dancer, into Gillian Lynne, a world-beating one.

I shared my disappointment by telephoning Nancy McNaught, who had been one of the head girls at Loddington Hall. She was very sympathetic to my burning desire to join a company like the Wells. Losing this chance felt like the end of my world. My mother's violent death on the eve of the war and my father's being in constant danger had instilled in me an impatience bordering on desperation. Also, emotions were high during these war years and I wanted to grab the chance offered to me, and not waste time. Nancy happened to be a family friend of Donald Albery, the administrator of the Sadler's Wells Ballet, and she contacted him on my behalf to arrange a meeting.

Without my aunt's or uncle's knowledge, I met Mr Albery

at his offices in what was then the New Theatre, before it became the Albery and then the Noël Coward. The office was at the hub of theatrical life in London – the New was the occasional home not only to the Sadler's Wells Ballet, but also to classical plays and dramas starring Laurence Olivier, Ralph Richardson and Alec Guinness. It has always been my favourite theatre – it is overflowing with the indefinable special warmth that creates the kind of theatre that is sure to make the blood race and the instinct and imagination buzz. Donald was a lean, saturnine man with intelligent eyes that seemed to see through to the back of your brain. His family had managed three of London's best theatres – the Wyndham, Criterion and New – and he had 'theatre' in every blood cell. He had a wicked sense of humour and this wailing passionate child pacing up and down in front of him must have made him chuckle. It was the beginning of a long friendship. From that day forward, way past my performing days and into my life as a director and choreographer, he was an adviser and friend.

At the end of the meeting he was kind and reassuring. 'Don't worry, Gillian, we will wait the six months until you are eighteen and then ask again. Do please keep in touch and I'll talk to Madam. And – don't despair.'

I bounced along Charing Cross Road and wondered how to tell my aunt and uncle about my unforgivable disobedience. So I telephoned Daddy instead. He was pleased but insisted, 'You must tell Auntie Bessie at once.' I suspect he was in touch with her immediately to smooth things over for me and when I got back to East Croydon she and Uncle Phil received me with warmth and pleasure, with not a 'how dare you' in sight. Perhaps they were both looking forward to coming and seeing me dance in such a famous company.

I studied hard for the next six months and Molly's studio in St John's Wood was virtually my home. Molly insisted I take the Advanced Cecchetti Ballet Exam, skipping all the previous grades, because she knew learning such a difficult syllabus would strengthen my technique. Gerd Larsen decided she'd like to have a go at it as well. This was great for both of us as by now we had become rivals, which proved extremely helpful when faced with a seemingly impossible series of pirouettes, or *renversés*, where the body has to do a twisting complete round turn while the legs balance sturdily as the body twists against them.

Gerd Larsen and me

Gerd and I enjoyed spurring each other on and this healthy competition made each of us try harder and get better. The syllabus was full of very detailed strengthening technical feats. Very few people we knew had taken the exam and I struggled with the demands of it. However, entirely thanks to Molly's knowledge and regime, I found the effort elating. And there were other rewards as well: I was allowed off one afternoon to go and see Malcolm Goddard, my friend from the Cone Ripman school, in *The Merry Widow* at His Majesty's. He danced beautifully in Lehár's fine operetta. The two leads were expertly played by Cyril Ritchard and Madge Elliot, a married couple from Australia, who were at the top of their game. I went backstage afterwards to see Malcolm and of course he introduced me to them. I felt very starry-eyed and proud of my friend, and found these two leading actors amusing and cheeky. The whole event was a great boost. A taste of a good production, in such a lovely theatre with all its history, was all I needed and when I returned to work the next day I surprised everybody with my zeal.

Back home in Croydon, our little wartime-created family was also working hard. My dear Auntie Bess had become very important and much respected in the bank, but she had to stand all day and, as she was a tall, strongly built woman, it was hard on her long legs and I saw that they gave her trouble at night. Uncle Phil was truly pulling his weight for the first time and always had a pot of tea ready for her as she sank thankfully into a comfortable chair after struggling home from work. He was doing well running all their acts – pianists, singers, cabaret artistes and stand-up comics – so we always had a lot to discuss at the end of the day. Refreshed by her tea my aunt, often without having taken off her hat or gloves, used to do the best she could with powdered eggs and a few vegetables for our dinner, along with bread when we could get it. And, looking back, I think that as I sat darning my *pointe* shoes (also hard to come by) and we listened to the news of the war, there may have been the odd nip of whisky or cognac donated from my grandfather's cellars to give a little bubble to my aunt's and uncle's evening.

Work at the studio continued relentlessly. Gerd and I were missing fewer pirouettes, our feet had quickened up considerably and we hardly ever fell over. Travis suggested to Molly that they should teach me *Casse Noisette* as performed by the Sugar Plum Fairy and I attacked the solo and its famous *pas de deux* with the new-found feeling of theatricality I'd taken away from my visit to His Majesty's. Indeed, Molly's prediction that the Advanced Cecchetti syllabus would strengthen the rest of my dancing proved correct, and I was able to relish Act Two of Ivanov's lovely choreography without feeling brought down by the technicalities. Tchaikovsky's beautiful *pas de deux* is incandescent and shimmering, and a joy to dance. I enjoyed it so much that Molly decided to include it in one of her Sunday lunchtime concerts so Travis and I could perform it. The Fairy's solo is light, speedy, with very intricate footwork. Again, Cecchetti's difficult centre-practice, which has similar requirements, had prepared the way.

'Travis,' I said before we went on, 'I am so fortunate. I'll never have another partner lift me so high and support me so well and look so lovingly at me!'

'Oh, yes you will, Gillian. We hope for great things for you, but maybe no one will enjoy partnering you as much as I do.'

I laughed at his sweetness. Together we were stylish, clean, accurate – and the hit of the afternoon.

The run of Malcolm's show had ended so he came to support me, wildly applauding in the process. Afterwards we snuck off to the London Palladium to see our school friend Margaret – Maggie – Roseby appearing in *Best Bib and Tucker*, which starred the great Tommy Trinder who was receiving attention for bringing the house down by appearing brilliantly as Carmen Miranda. Wendy Toye, who was the first female director-chore-ographer of note in England and also a very clever dancer, had held extensive auditions for the role of the Jackdaw, which she had based on the poem 'The Jackdaw of Rheims' by Richard Harris Barham. Hearing of the auditions, our school had sent Maggie up to London to try for the role and, wonderful dancer that she had become, she had secured it.

As we climbed up to the gods of that admired theatre, one of the very best in London, where the rapport between audi-ence and stage is second to none, we felt like becoming jackdaws ourselves – taking off way up near the roof and flying around our friend, so proud and thrilled were we at Maggie's much talked about star quality and brilliant reviews.

There were mugs of hot tea in her dressing room afterwards. I hugged her and said in her ear, 'Mags, you were wonderful!' Then Malcolm and I simultaneously said, 'You've become a star!'

Malcolm continued proudly, 'Was it amazingly hard to learn? I bet Miss Gracie must be thrilled?'

I added, 'Was it very hard to develop the stamina?'

'Not really, because Wendy is so inventive and such a hard taskmaster I never noticed how killing it was!' Maggie answered with her divine face smiling broadly.

I burst in about it being the same with Molly and Malcolm agreed, and we all three laughed the laughter that friends from childhood share. We were three happy people who lived for the theatre and as the theatre closed around us we promised to keep in touch – well, as much as the war would allow.

In a bolt out of the blue, Molly Lake decided to choreograph a pantomime and that I should be in it as the Principal Dancer – two shows daily would be excellent for stamina and also toughen me up. She chose *Cinderella*, which would go to Brixton for three weeks and then to Mansfield for two weeks. Not the most exhilarating places for theatre-going, I thought, but still, experience was invaluable and if Molly had told me to row to the Shetlands I would have done it.

Willie, another girl from Molly's, was also in the show, so here I was in the strange world of pantomime again – two years after being a Babe in Cambridge but in a slightly more elevated position. Willie and I found digs on St Saviour's Road, Brixton Hill, and Molly choreographed an unnecessarily difficult technical solo (I suppose she was using the whole thing as a training exercise) to an exotic piece from the opera *Faust*, which sounded strange from the wholly businesslike band we had, whose training had long been forgotten and whose lungs and fingers nearly collapsed with the effort.

Then suddenly Christmas was staring us in the face. Could Daddy possibly get leave? Could Aunt Bess cope with having us *and* still be able to do her work? How would I find the time to buy any presents? At least I was earning. The pantomime provided a steady seasonal salary, but December 1943 was a feverish and frantic time. We had all got used to the blackout by now – no street lamps, no lights of any kind showing and nothing that would give away a target for the Luftwaffe – but it added a slightly eerie atmosphere to everything.

Miraculously (or because of my firm belief that my mother was watching over me), Daddy did get two days' leave and I got away after the matinée on Christmas Eve. We had a heart-warming time at Addiscombe Road, my aunt was so welcoming and happy to have us with her and Uncle Phil was charming and funny, and my darling dearest daddy beamed from ear to ear the whole time. We all felt the presence of Mummy sending us her care and goodwill. On Christmas Day we walked round the corner to my grandfather's house on Radcliffe Road and sat at the large dining table where we were joined by my Uncle Sid (one of Mummy's brothers) and his neat adorable wife Nita. A chicken had been purloined, some potatoes and greens foraged from Grandpa's garden and my grandmother had even managed a trifle – a traditional English Christmas dinner in the middle of war. With Sid and Daddy representing Army and Air Force, Bessie a banker, Nita making clothes from nothing (she had worked at Chanel before the war), Grandpa and his gardening, Grandma making meals from nothing and I, a panto-mime soloist and aspiring ballerina, we were a motley crew whose happiness at being able to get together was heightened by the war. Again, I felt Mummy's nearness, not that she was there with us, but that she was meshing us together in some way.

The rest of the holiday I spent happily clinging to Daddy and laughing with Auntie Bess and Uncle Phil. But it ended all too soon and we dashed back to our various workplaces – in my case slightly plumper than when I'd left, which didn't please me. We worked hard to regain our regime and sell our show to the Brixton populace. Molly visited and gave us all piercingly accurate notes – especially me – and the show began to pick up. The bosses of Moss Empire, who ran the London Hippodrome and many other theatres, popped in and thank goodness that show went well and we even got some cheers.

On New Year's Day I wrote to Daddy thanking him for his presents and for fighting to get leave so he could be with us in Croydon:

Our landlady is still feeding us excellently, we've had chicken, and pears, liver and bacon and all sorts of lovely things. Willie and I got quite desperate just before 12, because we were determined to drink the New Year in with something – but we hadn't anything. At the last moment we drank, at my suggestion, Andrews Liver Salts, a gulp to each stroke of the 12 o'clock – it was better than nothing. Then just as we put our glasses down, in came Mrs Joy with the port-wine – we could have kicked ourselves. Still it was better late than never. At the theatre we sang 'Auld Land Syne' and joined up with the audience, and then we all sang 'God save the King'. Sometimes I feel that I ought not to be so happy dancing. I feel I ought to be doing something more useful: but at least dancing gives pleasure to people and it helps them forget their worries for a while – so maybe I'm more useful in that, than by doing anything else.

We reached the end of our season in Brixton having done reasonably well and learnt a lot more about life in the commercial theatre. Our first lesson was the need, with two shows a day, for endless workouts. I had gone in mid morning each day when we could usually get a clear stage, joined by Willie, to keep up with our daily class. (It is easier to drive oneself if there is another person sweating away so neither of you can give in.) As my dances were showy and difficult this necessitated another barre session just before each show so that the muscles were very warm, and thus I dropped into a routine that was to become all too familiar: three workouts per day plus performances, the two-show-a-day ritual. Then there was the dirt! The wings behind the scenery, where I often had to hang on to an old pipe, had certainly not been scrubbed for some time and as my feet brushed over the boards they threw up considerable dust. The band, a very jolly bunch of old chaps – the young ones were at war and no women seemed to have penetrated their ranks – were full of zest, but their tempi were erratic. And thus began a lifetime of dialogues with various conductors small and grand, and in this case our musical director. Often I started with a mixture of polite request followed by examples: 'Can't you see it is impossible to do these endless pirouettes round the stage to a tempo that would beat an express train?'

This would lead to pleading and, as a last resort, a hug and a laugh. I hadn't yet learnt the best method – flirtation – though. I also learnt to respect the will and energy of variety performers, and their bonhomie and generosity, and certainly I learnt to appreciate their often ribald humour and enjoyed many laughs of a most unballetic kind.

We packed up and off we went to the mining town of

Mansfield, our full company on the train with the stage manager going up and down the platform checking we were all assembled. Willie and I had written ahead and arranged our digs, which turned out to be in a large house that had seen better times. We had to climb steep stairs to our rooms and noticed at least two slightly ominous-looking men in the large living room as we passed. It became clear that Willie and I were very different from the usual guests, and while the landlady was stalwart and friendly we did find ourselves fending off lewd suggestions on the staircase as we climbed up to our rooms after the show.

Three days before the end of my stay one of the men, Harry, presented me with a book wrapped in plain brown paper. 'I heard yer name was Gillian, so Gillian 'ere's summat for yer. I thought yer ought to be readin' summat like this. Help yer understand life a bit more. So 'ere's my present for a beautiful dancer who oughta be livin' a bit!'

He placed the parcel in my hands and I thanked him firmly saying, 'I'll have time to read it when the panto is over. Thank you very much for thinking of me.' I was quite proud of my present until I delved into the first chapters and realised it was really rather racy and therefore perhaps not quite for me, so I saved it to give to my father (rather to his surprise).

We left Mansfield much stronger in stamina and having survived the dosshouse and its pitfalls. Molly's wisdom in sending me off on that unlikely journey had paid off, it had opened my eyes to all sorts of aspects of life that were utterly new to me and therefore my personality as a performer became much more interesting. Now it was back to the rigid discipline of St John's Wood to correct the inevitable faults in technique and line that had slipped in. Molly's demands became stronger than ever. She would accept nothing less than one hundred per cent of each move, however impossible.

Life was so busy I failed to notice that the six-month wait my aunt had insisted on when she had spoken with Madam de Valois was almost up. Molly started on a new ballet and we celebrated my eighteenth birthday on Sunday, 20 February 1944, at my grandpa's house. He and I took a turn round the garden together even though it was cold. This was a treasured ritual for us both and as always we felt sad that his adored Barbara, my mother, could not be with us.

The following morning, early, the telephone rang and I heard Auntie say, 'Good morning, Addiscombe 3587. Yes, of course my niece is here. You just caught her. Who's speaking, please?' As I rushed downstairs she whispered, 'It's a Mr Albery for you.'

I took the telephone from her and said, 'Hello, this is Gillian.'

'Good morning, Gillian, it's Donald Albery here. Happy birthday for yesterday. I hope you had a good time?'

'Yes, thank you,' I mumbled nervously.

'I rang to tell you that our offer still stands and we would like you to join our company. What do you say?'

I just about managed to say, 'Wait a minute, Mr Albery, would you?' And turning to my Auntie Bess I whispered, 'They want me to join the company.'

My aunt stood open-mouthed, then smiled and said, 'Oh, darling.'

'Thank you very much, Mr Albery, I'd be delighted!' was all I could manage to gasp into the phone.

'Oh, that is good news, Gillian. We would like you to present yourself at ten o'clock sharp for class on Monday at Sadler's Wells Theatre on Rosebery Avenue. We shall look forward to seeing you then. Good luck!' And he hung up.

I looked at my dear aunt and we ran towards each other and hugged, laughing and crying. I'm not sure either of us had really believed it would ever happen.

Mummy's dreams for me were coming true.

Ready

SEVEN

Sadler's Wells Ballet

1944

Displaying my Classical Greek line

O N THE MORNING OF 27 March 1944 I alighted from the No. 38 bus and walked along Rosebery Avenue and past the partially reconstructed Sadler's Wells Theatre. First built as a music house in 1683, over monastic waters discovered in Richard Sadler's garden, the 'Sadler's Wells' miraculous cures were part of the theatre's original draw but a raucous type of entertainment subsequently flourished there, attracting an alternative London crowd. By the late 1920s the theatre was in a shabby state. But then Lilian Baylis stepped in, campaigning tirelessly to save Sadler's Wells for the nation – so successfully that the theatre was rebuilt by Frank Matcham and opened in

1931. It had been bombed in 1940 and had been closed ever since, but the rehearsal rooms were intact and very much in use.

Having only ever entered the theatre through the foyer, this time I walked straight up to the stage door and presented myself to the doorman, who peered at me quite kindly. 'Hello, I'm new, I'm coming to join the company' – chin proudly going up a notch – 'and I need to find the dressing room to change into my practice clothes.'

'Right, Miss, go through those doors. Turn right, take the lift to the fifth floor, go through the Ballet Room and it will be there down a couple of stairs, all right?'

'Yes, thank you.'

'Good luck,' he said.

My heart was thumping as I approached the lift and began my journey. Thank God I was very early, as I'd never have had the courage to cross that Ballet Room to get to the dressing room if there'd been anyone there. As I was changing, the room started to fill up and the chatter grew and grew, and I got smaller and smaller. On the way back to the Ballet Room I was stopped by a very tall, elegant, jolly and forthright girl. 'You're new, what's your name?'

'Well, actually Jill Pyrke, but they've changed it to Gillian Lynne,' I said.

'Just as well,' said Moyra Fraser, who became a watchful friendly eye from then on. 'What are those things on the side of your head?'

'They're hairgrips to hold my hair back.' (I had a lot of dark hair coming to just above my shoulders.) I was now definitely feeling inadequate.

'Well, we don't *wear* hairgrips, Gillian,' and she whipped them out and away. 'You've got lovely hair; tie it back and you'll be fine,' and off she went.

I scrabbled about in my work bag, the one thing that never leaves a dancer's side, and found a hair band. Shaking, I scraped my hair back. Then, with a deep breath I pushed open the doors and entered the rehearsal room, as a member of the Sadler's Wells Ballet. There, with her back towards me, was the divine, familiar figure of the ballerina of the company, Margot Fonteyn, warming up and stretching on the barre. I could hardly breathe as the thought hit me, 'I am going to dance in the same room as Margot Fonteyn.'

Margot Fonteyn

I was rooted to the spot as she turned to face me and stretched her other leg. She gave me a huge welcoming smile. Margot's smile was famous – a strong, sudden sunbeam that bathed its recipient in light. I found my legs and ran to stash my bag under the piano like everyone else. Then the doors swung open and Ninette de Valois swept in at a clip – she never ambled.

'Good morning, everyone, straight to the barre, please.' Within seconds the barres were all occupied. She saw my hesitancy and said, 'Lynne, go between Fonteyn and May!' and as I slipped into the little space made for me by Margot and Pamela May she said, 'Lynne is going to join our company,' and without pause rattled off her first instructions. I had time, before the *pliés*, to catch a little helpful smile of approval from Moyra Fraser across the room – she had spotted my hair band.

What a day, what happiness, how decent everyone was and how hard I tried! I had never jumped as high in my life and, in arabesque, my leg shot up until it was nearly vertical. So high, in fact, that Madam yelled, 'Lynne, lower that leg – there is no need to touch the ceiling. You are disturbing your line.'

The weeks that followed my first lovely day were crammed with getting to know who was who and learning steps in all the current works in the company's repertoire, the 'full-lengthers' and selections it was due to perform in its forthcoming season. This was further complicated because I was now learning corps de ballet steps and not the principal parts I had been used to. Of course it was hard coming down from being Molly's lead dancer and doing only solo roles to being one of many dancers in a totally supportive position, but at Sadler's Wells everyone new had to join in the corps de ballet and I didn't expect anything else. Nevertheless, I inwardly gave myself one year maximum to be noticed and climb up off the bottom rung.

Gerd Larsen and I rehearsing
Lac des Cygnes, *1944*

So I got on with it. In *Lac des Cygnes* I was one of many swans and townsfolk; in *Giselle* one of a shroud of ethereal dead maidens, or Wili, in the second act; in Robert Helpmann's dramatic, interesting *Hamlet* I learnt to be a court lady; in Ninette de Valois's *Promenade* I was a cheeky peasant girl full of character with sickled (turned-in) feet; and in Frederick

Ashton's *Les Rendezvous*, which to this day is one of my favourite pieces of choreography – it is difficult and brilliantly musical with a delicious score by Auber arranged by Sadler's Wells composer-conductor Constant Lambert – I was part of the interwoven ensemble. I thought I had died and gone to heaven.

Very soon after I had joined the company we set off on a tour of England. Ballet companies, like most theatrical enterprises, spent a lot of their time touring the provincial theatres not just presenting their London seasons. The somewhat beleaguered population of the metropolis could not have supported them for very long, therefore touring the country was financially necessary. Our first stop was the Wimbledon Theatre, where I overheard Peggy van Praagh saying to Madam, 'Thank goodness we have got hold of Gillian.'

I wondered how I could possibly live up to their faith in me but proudly performed my Peasant and Swan in *Lac des Cygnes* as the newest member of Sadler's Wells Ballet.

Being on tour intensified everything. It was the perfect introduction to my new life. I felt happy at last. All the sadness I had experienced since 1939, all the uncertainty, all the longing, suddenly turned round as I became someone who was arriving and believing and finding her path. In my diary I added Sadler's Wells Ballet as my second *home* address. Travelling around the country in such close proximity, I felt that the company was my new family. It was an extraordinary group of people. The company was interesting because it was created before the days when the size and shape of limbs had to comply with some idea of regimented perfection. To keep her company alive, Madam had sometimes to take in people who were *not* physically perfect but who were rich in other things – their acting ability, large personality, unusual speed or odd technical feats – and those who could learn and produce versatile stage-craft quickly. Her company was polyglot, full of individuals with diverse personalities and talents. It made for very good theatre and a lot of excitement backstage.

Margot and Pamela took me under their wing immediately and offered advice – and sometimes admonitions – daily. And then there was David Paltenghi whom I already knew from Molly Lake's studio. He loved literature and was altogether delicious. Seeing him every day I fell instantly under his spell, but sadly he was in a relationship with a little, sharp, clever technician and free spirit called Joan Sheldon. There was Alexis Rassine from Lithuania, who was very young and hand-some, and Margaret Dale, who was highly intelligent and a snappy, smart dancer. I also instantly became friends with Henry Danton, an original, fascinating dancer with a pale, serious, attractive face. Henry had started dancing late but, with his perfect physique, he had taken to the art naturally. He also had more brains than most. He was a special person and later on I would have the pleasure of being partnered by him a lot.

Henry Danton

Robert Helpmann, our star male dancer, was Australian. The rumour was that when Madam had auditioned him in the thirties she had not been knocked out by his dancing but had exclaimed, 'That face! I can do something with that face.' It was a face made for the theatre. Bobby was an actor-dancer in the ballet, an actor in the straight theatre and he had simultaneously worked with Laurence Olivier on films while performing in live theatre. He was fun, clever as paint and knew how to bamboozle the audience into thinking his technique was very strong, when it was not. He too was a wonderful partner.

Frederick Ashton, choreographer of ravishingly beautiful ballets, was also fascinating, especially to famous and stylish women. Although Fred was gay, he was sexually irresistible to women. He had a languidly stylised way of talking, he reeked of class and there was always a glimmer of self-awareness and humour behind his eyes. His choreography is intensely musical, lyrical yet daring; it is very fulfilling to dance, yet subtly difficult. He occasionally danced in some of his own ballets and his performances were always witty and charming. He took an interest in me immediately and soon I was lucky enough to be in all his works.

There was also a familiar face from my Madeleine Sharp schooldays: sixteen-year-old Beryl Grey, the company's brilliant youngest ballerina, was already established as an extraordinary dancer for one so young. She had grown very tall and had a powerful physical strength on stage. She was handsome, like a great stallion, with that kind of elegance and beauty. Her technique was already formidable and she and I often talked about our first days in the world of dance. My other soulmate, who became a lifelong friend too, was Moira Shearer. Tall, with skin as white as a dove's feather and flaming electric-red hair, she was also a strong technician. Audiences were in awe of her beauty and eager men queued up to speak to her wherever we went.

Moira Shearer

After Wimbledon we set off for Newcastle's Theatre Royal, then to Hammersmith and on to Bournemouth, then back to the New Theatre, just one of the Wells's temporary theatre homes in London, for a long summer season. We began work on a new ballet, Andrée Howard's *Le Festin de l'Araignée* (Spider's Banquet), with music by Roussel, in which I was cast as an Ant. Never has such an insignificant-sounding role been such a source of pride. Andrée was very specific about what she wanted from us, had a magical sense of characterisation and showed remarkable patience with my overeager enquiring ant. One day during technical rehearsals we were all trooping off to lunch, still in costume, through the pass door and up to one of the small bars, when I saw a beetle-shell leaning against the wall. I took no notice of the costume until Madam called, 'Where's Nye? Where's Palma Nye?'

As an ant in Le Festin de l'Araignée, *1944*

I ran down the stairs to where I had seen the beetle, peered inside, rushed back up to the bar and said, 'Excuse me, Madam, but Nye's on the landing, she's fainted inside her shell.'

Everyone zoomed down to witness Nye's resuscitation and subsequent embarrassment. There was a lot of laughter and Palma was not allowed to forget it for a long time.

We opened *Le Festin* on 20 June 1944. It was a fun start for me. I was in awe of everything but was especially taken with the beauty of Moira Shearer emerging from a chrysalis as the Butterfly and Pauline Clayden's brilliance and speed as a Dragonfly.

During these weeks of touring and learning two girls became really good friends to me. Dancers are usually very helpful to newcomers trying to learn the ballets, but these two were more than that and they schooled me in the company habits and procedures, which were daunting. One was Paula Dunning, known for some reason as Topsy, who was stunningly beautiful with high, plump cheekbones and huge eyes. She was never going to be a big soloist but she was a good actress and you couldn't take your eyes off her sweet appearance – and her nature was as sweet as her looks. The other was Lorna Mossford – Mossie – who could not have been more different. She was razor thin with a bony, slim face and a brilliantly fast technique. Highly practical and neat – she kept meticulous diaries – she was also very caring. We began to eat together, shared every experience, helped each other and became the closest of pals.

Throughout the assimilation process Margot and Pamela continued to go out of their way to check I was all right. Whenever we had time to chat they would gently probe me on the circumstances of Mummy's death, how it had affected me and Daddy, the life I'd led since the crash, how and where I'd lived. Margot's mother, Mrs Hookham – named the Black Queen by one and all – was very strong and they were very close. She was Margot's guiding hand – powerful, outspoken and compelling – and I think Margot felt sorry for me having no such influence in my life. She must have said something to her mother for from then on the Black Queen also took an interest in me, giving me advice on hair and make-up: 'I'd wear that hair scraped back a bit more, darling! And do try and wear the same colour tights and top when you can. You'll look better and you'll stand out more. Keep your eye on Margot, especially the arms. You have long slim arms, very good, but you can learn a lot from the fluidity in Margot's arms.'

I all but curtseyed as I replied, 'Oh, thank you, Black Queen. I'll try to do exactly as you say.' Margot was our top ballerina and her mother a grand and powerful figure. She was also very striking with her shining black eyes and grey-white hair.

Pamela offered warmth and love, and used to ask, 'So there is no lovely man in your life yet?' And, 'Our boys like you a lot, Lynne, you should go out sometimes!'

I did not admit to my useless passion for David, which was

exacerbated by the present he had given me of a bound edition of Milton's *Paradise Lost* inscribed lovingly as a welcome to the company. I was reading it avidly in bed at night and my thoughts ranged wildly into imaginings perhaps closer to the book Harry had given me as a hopeful inducement, and which was now resting in my father's strongbox. It was all heady wine for this hopeless romantic.

Back from our tour, we found the Germans had unleashed their fiendish secret weapon – the V1 flying bombs, or doodle-bugs as they became known. I was still living with Auntie Bess and Uncle Phil in East Croydon, one of the most bombed places in England, so going up and down to London was hazardous, especially at night. Often the train had to stop, the passengers like sitting ducks, bombs exploding to right and left; then, when our nerves had been thoroughly shaken, it would pick itself up and diddley-dum, diddley-dum, diddley-dum on to East Croydon and beyond. For some curious reason we were not really frightened. I was too young, I suppose, and life in the ballet had at last given me an artistic home, so perhaps my happiness drove out the fear.

At the New Theatre in St Martin's Lane the redoubtable Donald Albery, my knight in shining armour, oversaw the company from his small office. We had doodlebug spotters on the roof as we got ready and during our performances. Because I was eighteen and a junior member of the company, my dressing room was always at the top. The spotters would patrol the roof, binoculars at the ready, and as soon as a doodlebug was sighted in the distance they would give one blast on a whistle. This put us on our mettle but we continued putting on our make-up; if the bomb came near and/or towards us, there would be multiple whistles and, swearing, we'd take to the stairs – considered to be the safest place to be during bombing – mirrors in hand. We continued with our greasepaint and waited, either until the bug passed over or, if it cut out near us, for the shattering crash as it dropped like a stone. We had no time for fear, the show had to go on. We'd go directly back up to our dressing rooms and carry on, thankful that it hadn't been our turn this time, but also inwardly grieving for the poor people who hadn't been so lucky. Bombs, danger, ruined streets, no food to speak of – these were commonplace

Les Sylphides

to us. The discipline of the dancer was such that we seemed to sail through it. Somehow the hard work and joy of performing shielded us from the horror.

At the New Theatre, on 13 July 1944, in the worst of the flying bomb period that summer, we were dancing *Les Sylphides*. Our orchestra consisted of Constant Lambert ably assisted by Hilda Gaunt. The two of them were playing a grand piano each, arranged facing each other in the orchestra pit, which had been raised so we could hear them and they could see us – and each other. The air-raid sirens had been going off all day, and we started the performance knowing it would be a rocky night.

Les Sylphides, one of Fokine's greatest ballets, starts with a beautiful group, tight and very together. The prima ballerina and her partner are in the middle, the soloists who will perform the waltz, mazurka and prelude solos are in front of them on their knees and the corps de ballet form a semicircle – four a side – which cocoons the principals. When the curtain goes up it reveals a calm and geometric beauty. However, one of our ballerina's nerves always resulted in uncomfortable wind – which she usually had to relieve just before the stage manager gave his instruction for the curtain to rise. Consequently, our calm and beautiful group that night was actually struggling desperately to hold their giggles in check as the curtain slowly went up.

It was a particularly shaky evening as far as awful crashes and thumps were concerned, and despite their best efforts Constant and Hilda could not quite drown out the noise. There is a moment in the ballet where the entire corps turns to face upstage, arms softly undulating; it is a tranquil, hovering hiatus, with emotions held in. That night, at that precise moment, a doodlebug could unmistakably be heard getting nearer and nearer, louder and louder. Nobody dared breathe, not the company, nor our gallant orchestra of two, nor the audience, and to our horror it sounded as if the flying bomb had cut out right above us. The usual tranquil, hovering pause was extended and extended, all arms stock still, feet *en pointe* riveting us to the floor, necks strained, listening, the terrible silence reigning. Then came a huge and dreadful crash coupled with a sickening noise nearby, and with relief Constant and Hilda launched into the next section passionately and far too fast. We shot into the next few bars – over-dancing, arms extravagantly waving – so relieved the bomb hadn't landed on us. In fact, it had come down in St Martin's Lane, just beyond the theatre, with devastating results. We were very, very lucky.

When we left via the stage door that night, Mossie and I held hands and walked down Cecil Court to St Martin's Lane. We couldn't believe the sad scene further up the street. Ambulances, air-raid workers, Home Guard soldiers and Londoners were all in the middle of the smoking rubble trying to help the people who had been injured. How had the bomb missed us? We were moved and grateful that we were standing there unharmed. The jagged, ugly scene before us was so far from the gentle lyrical whiteness of *Les Sylphides*, which had immersed us minutes before. The street had become burnt orange in colour – with metal cranes, ambulances, black-coated Home Guards, the military and police all pitching in to help extricate people from the smoke. Acrid smells of burning wafted up the street from the crater created by the deadly bomb. The atmosphere was full of smoke, colour and noise – the wails of agony, the cries of assurance from the helpers, the squeal of the crane's mechanism as it lifted firefighters aloft to smother the remaining flames. But the powerful effort to help those injured and buried filled the air with positivity, *not* defeat. Mossie and I held on to an injured girl caught in the blast before handing her over to someone with medical experience and then decided to find somewhere to get a cup of something hot and comforting. We could not just go home, we were far too churned up, and besides, the all clear had not been sounded. Over coffee and a treat of an iced bun we picked over what we had just seen and also the night's performance. When the all clear sounded we were more than ready to make our way to our beds.

It seems incredible to me now how easily we took the danger and often horror in our stride. And also how, in spite of the rationing, which was just getting worse and worse – unless you were filthy rich and could go on the Black Market – we seemed to eat a lot and often, although the food was pretty basic. I can only assume that the quality of each meal was of such limited calorific worth when set against the enormous energy we had to expend – on average we danced, with class rehearsals and performances, eight and a half hours per day – that little and often it had to be. When time would allow there were visits to Beoty's, an Italian restaurant just near the theatre, Vega, a vegetarian place on Leicester Square, or the Lyons Corner House at Piccadilly. Lunches at Beoty's, which I usually had with Moira, were always the same, we couldn't have afforded more even if they had had it: soup, a roll with margarine, tomato and cheese. Tea with Moira, Mossie or Topsy after rehearsal and before the show was taken at the Vega: tea with milk, then toast with jam and cream whipped on to it. I doubt that the cream was real, but to us

Ninette de Valois

it was an unmitigated luxury. At the Lyons Corner House we were able miraculously to find hot chocolate – it must have been powdered milk – and very occasionally a *pain au raisin*. None of this food was much good for dancing and most of it was fattening, but at this stage of the war getting fat was *not* a problem.

Throughout, we were guided, ruled, helped and led by our remarkable 'Madam'. As the years went on, and certainly the minute I started choreographing and directing myself, I became more and more aware of what incredible good fortune it was almost to have been brought up by Madam. She was a brilliant – and very beautiful, very creative, very tough, charismatic and inspiring – leader. Most of us were more than a little afraid of her. I definitely was, but only because I wanted to be marvellous *for* her.

Her staging and choreography were wonderful to dance, and rewarding too. And meaty – you could get your teeth into it. Of course, sometimes we thought her unfair and the familiar dancer's moan from my Molly's studio days could often be heard at the Wells too. A dancer's daily work is hard, perhaps even painful, and sometimes it helps to complain. 'My back's as stiff as a ramrod today', 'I bruised my toenail in those awful worn-out *pointe* shoes, and I can't find my arnica', 'What does Madam think I am, a tank?', 'Why don't we rehearse all night as well as all day?' . . . and so on. None of it is deeply serious, but it helps to ease the true rigours of being a ballet dancer. Tincture of arnica was a lifesaver for our bruised toenails, often incurred during strenuous work in *pointe* shoes past their prime. My method of applying it was to find an old pair of socks, soak two pieces of cotton wool in the arnica, wrap them across my toenails, put the socks on to hold them in place and then sleep in them. It stained the sheets and certainly wasn't very attractive, but it took the bruising out in one night.

Madam called me either Lynne (we were usually addressed by our surnames) or 'the smiler'. Sometimes she gave pulverisingly difficult classes but they were always fun, and fiendishly detailed. You could feel the vibrations of all the grumblings that were going on under the breath, especially from the boys, who liked to show off their big lunges and jumps as she set her fast, intricate *enchaînements*, which were often impossibly difficult to dance, but were nevertheless much easier for girls than for boys. But her wit meant some of her remarks as she cut us down to size were very funny, so there would be laughter along with the anxiety and of course everyone wanted to impress her always, whatever they said. It was a nerve-racking time but absolutely exhilarating.

Back in East Croydon Auntie Bess coped with my changing moods of fantastical optimism or abject despair as they came. I think she still recognised a lot of Mummy in me but I must have been a handful since all serious dancers seem to live in a world of their own and are not always easy to deal with. I continued to journey up and down between Victoria and East Croydon and, just as the bombs were a familiar part of life, so was devastation, danger and uncertainty, so she was always relieved to have me home and be able to give me a hug. One night I arrived a little late as the train had had to stop longer than usual, high up on its vulnerable tracks, while the German venom crashed down to the right and left of us. We would be in for a bad night. Auntie took one look at my rather drained face and said, 'Right, Phil, pack a few things up, we are going round to Grandpa's!'

I knew she was right, I felt exhausted from dancing and rehearsing all day, they had both been worried about me and she had had a day of dealing with perpetually shocked people – customers and staff alike – at the bank. The comforting solidity of a house like Shirleyhurst, which offered a little more security than 241 Addiscombe Road or the Anderson shelter opposite, was a sensible solution. We grabbed our toothbrushes and next day's clothes – practice and *pointe* shoes for me – and Auntie yelled upstairs to Mr Richards, 'Tommy! We are going round the corner to my father's house. Please come and use the basement. It looks like it is going to be bad!'

Off we went scurrying round into Radcliffe Road to my grandfather's. My grandparents had gone to bed but let us in, kissed us and went back to their room. Auntie and I went upstairs to one of the spare bedrooms and Uncle Phil played darts against himself in the big room adjoining the cellar, which now had mats, blankets, pillows and spare eiderdowns in it. Auntie and I had only just got undressed when the lethal drone of an advancing V1 flying monstrosity filled the air. Up we shot, and down the two flights of stairs to the basement. Three huge explosions followed but the thick walls of Shirleyhurst cushioned us well and we decided to stay down there. The bombing carried on relentlessly for another two hours and then I got really angry at it. I couldn't sleep and my limbs needed a proper bed.

'I'm going back up to my bed. I don't care if five bombs crash down on us at once. I've got to try and sleep – at least I won't know anything about it!' I declared belligerently. And I stomped off back upstairs, feeling cross, spoilt and rather selfish, but extremely grateful to have a mattress under me. I'd been there ten minutes and was beginning to give in to sleep when what sounded like twenty monstrosities roaring full pelt approached and started cutting out and crashing one after the other. I was out of bed and down those stairs at the speed of light, and fell into my aunt's arms. She avoided saying I told you so, but we couldn't help bursting out laughing when Uncle Phil, looking across the candlelit space, offered a laconic, 'Staying down now, are we, Jill?'

In the following weeks we would hear that that particular night held the record for the number of V1 flying bombs dropped on Croydon.

We finished our season at the New Theatre in early August,

elated by the amazing audiences who braved the blackout, imperfect transport and danger everywhere to give us heart-warming receptions night after night, and we were also bolstered by feeling that we had been useful in terms of the war effort. In spite of the lack of lights in the streets, the fans would gather at the stage door to speak to us and it felt good to see how much we were cheering them up.

The doodlebugs had been falling all summer without a break, so a holiday was called for the company. I stayed in Croydon for a week to gather my thoughts before going down to Sussex to be near Daddy. I'd been so busy learning new choreography and trying to become a professional there'd been no time to see anyone else – none of my auntie's friends or Daddy's – so now it was good to be able to do some normal things, like meet my aunt at the bank, have a little snack lunch, chat to our Anderson shelter friends, have a look in the shops in Croydon, realise I had no coupons to buy anything with, tidy up my small room and then joyfully head off for Sussex. Daddy seemed very busy but also happy and he came to stay at the welcoming old Norfolk Arms in Arundel so we could have more time together.

I had always been mad about the sea and swimming, but there were very few swimming spots left since most of the south coast had been laid with mines. I badgered Daddy to find me a safe place on one of the beaches in his area. He drove us down to the beautiful beach at Climping. There were

'Danger' signs everywhere so I carefully put down my bag containing costume, towel and book. The shore and country down there were totally unspoilt; it was a warm summer's day and just the perfect spot for a dedicated seasider. Daddy could feel my impatience. I listened intently as he pointed out the only – rather narrow – passage where it was safe to swim.

'I'll stay here while you go in. But remember, Jill, you can only swim between this stone and that,' pointing to two markers on the beach, 'and keep to a straight line out and a straight line back. Do not deviate right or left! I'll stay here while you show me and once I know you are okay I have to get back to the aerodrome but I'll come back for you in a little while.' I leapt into my swimsuit and, rather gingerly it must be admitted, took to the water. Feeling nervous but not wanting to show it, I swam out about a hundred yards in a straight line, turned on the spot and waved. Luckily there was no undertow, otherwise I would have been in trouble. Daddy called out, 'Right, you've got it, now promise that's all you'll do. Come in soon and read your book and then I'll be back!'

When the English summer deigns to give us a warm sunny day it is second to none and the empty beach, with its seagulls gently soaring and the sea swirling languidly was idyllic . . . except for the 'Danger High Explosives' signs that encouraged me to return to the shore rather quickly when I realised I had forgotten which rock was the marker. I had a heavenly time and was totally dried, dressed and reading my book by the time my father returned. The look on his face when he saw that I had actually survived was a picture.

My dream had come true: I was now a true-blue member of the ballet. Not all dreams work out well, but mine was as gratifying and exhilarating as I'd imagined. Sure it was hard work, with moments of fear and disappointment: a ballet company is a very competitive world to exist in. But feelings of inadequacy were driven away by the euphoria of a performance going well and I knew that on such occasions I had been noticed with approval. I also became aware that my feelings towards the opposite sex were changing – becoming strong and exciting, or potentially so. Although I considered myself to be plain, my eyes and legs my only possible sources of beauty, I understood that something in me was clearly attractive to men and that they usually took an interest in me. I didn't bother to work it out, I only realised that Mummy's instruction about guarding my virginity might become more and more difficult to fulfil.

This sense of romance was probably enhanced by my frequent trips to the cinema – 1944 produced some very fine films, some gorgeous actors and actresses whose names were to last for many years and some sinuous and romantic scores. One film knocked me for six and still does. Laurence Olivier's magnificent *Henry V*. It was directed and acted by Olivier, a combination that is the trickiest of all technical feats to achieve and the downfall of many actors, and had a very beautiful score by William Walton. Before I joined Sadler's Wells I'd seen Frederick Ashton's ballet *The Quest*, which also has an exhilarating score by Walton, and from that day he became one of my most cherished composers. We all rushed to see the film as our very own Robert Helpmann was playing the Bishop of Ely in it. Somehow this made us feel very close to it, almost as if we'd contributed. Olivier had cast some of the most talented actors in England, Robert Newton and Ralph Richardson among them. He also found an English actress with a French-sounding name, Renée Asherson, to play Katherine. Her accent was so adorable that half of London went around quoting her.

On my return from holiday I had hurriedly to learn the 'Waltz' from *Façade*, and give several performances of the 'Mazurka' in *Coppelia* before we shot off for three weeks in Manchester. I felt at home in that friendly red-brick city from day one. It was the start of my lifelong affection for industrial buildings, great chimneys, warehouses and canals. I find them beautiful because they make strong statements visually, and represent the human zeal and fortitude of the people who throng into them every morning, and give of their guts and spirit all day before leaving at night. I far prefer this to some pretty town with no deep purpose. On top of this, Manchester had a marvellous opera house, with a great stage, a welcoming auditorium, elegant portals, a good backstage feel in the dressing rooms and wings, and the magic one hopes for hovering over its stage. We all enjoyed our time there, despite the fact that our digs in Acker Street, with their mean beds and rough edges, took a bit of getting used to.

We returned to London to start work on the new Robert Helpmann ballet *Miracle in the Gorbals* with a score by Arthur Bliss. We opened on 26 October 1944 at the Prince's Theatre (now the Shaftesbury). This was the first new ballet I had worked on with Helpmann, who had liked me from the start because he was such a wonderful actor and I was interested in acting and relished the dramatic roles. It was less a conventional, classical ballet, more a 'dance drama', and not only had Robert choreographed and staged it, he would also direct and star in it.

Bobby was wonderful to work with for three reasons. First, he seemed able to transform ordinary life into dance – this ballet was about the ordinary people in the Gorbals in Glasgow. It was the first ballet I'd ever done like that. Second, he was good at directing acting, which was rare in the ballet, and he made all the movements make sense because everything was invested with subtext. And third, he had a heightened sense of theatricality and was an amazing presence on stage. Although there were many better technical dancers, Bobby had that rare thing that meant that when he walked on stage you looked at little else. He also had a huge sense of humour, so rehearsals with him were exciting and funny. He had a wicked way of disguising the fact that he was not a great technician, especially when it came to pirouettes. He would make the preparation a thing of immense importance and then, doing only two turns, he would 'spot' four times on the way round, making you think he'd whipped off twice as many turns as he actually had. A master showman!

His ballet was about the rebirth of Christ into modern-day society, in this case the slums of Glasgow. Bobby played 'the stranger' – Christ, that is – and his passions and subsequent demise gave the ballet the feeling of a modern morality play without the words. I was cast as one of the women in the streets and 'first cast' to cover one of the Young Lovers, danced by Shearer and the elegant classical dancer Alexis Rassine. (Ballet companies, like opera companies, always have several separate casts to cover the important roles. It is a safeguard against injury, or sore throats in the case of opera, and also is a way of developing emerging talent.)

It was a wonderful ballet, earthy and of its time, and held together with powerful dynamics by Bliss's score. We all adored performing it. The choreography and the staging were entirely different and possibly more theatrical than anything else in the repertoire at the time. We could let go and get lost physically and mentally in the story.

At the King's Theatre in Hammersmith, Daddy came to visit on leave. I felt hugely proud as I looked out of my dressing-room window and there was my gallant father in his uniform on the pavement waving up at me. This was the first time he had seen me dance with such a large company and he looked relieved that his energetic child had finally landed happily.

I was lucky to be on as the girl lover the night Daddy was out front. Alexis was good to dance with and we enjoyed presenting our romantic lovers – a lyrical beam of hope cutting through the rough and sordid streets. Travis's teaching helped me feel relaxed and confident with Alexis during the *pas de deux*. My father not only liked the ballet but was pleased to see that I was on my way to becoming a soloist, and that made me even more proud.

At this time we were called in dribs and drabs to the headquarters of ENSA to be fitted up for uniforms for the up-and-coming Sadler's Wells Ballet Company tour to Belgium and France. I was really excited at the thought of being in khaki like my dad, and relieved as well. My very limited wardrobe of winter clothes was definitely not adequate for the sophistication of the Continent. We knew it would be freezing so the thought of the heavy uniform was a reassuring one.

After the Normandy landings, the Germans had been driven out of northern Europe by the Allied forces. It seemed incredible, but ENSA could now send artists to perform in what had so recently been occupied Europe: we were going to dance in Brussels, Paris, Ghent, Bruges and Ostend, entertaining English and American soldiers and airmen. This in itself was very exciting, and made us feel as if we were at last really part of the war effort, but on top of that I was about to go abroad for the first time. The very thought of Paris and Brussels, distant magical names, meant my usual sleep patterns became totally frenetic. What a world was about to open up for our company! I dreamed of architecture, new languages, unusual food and felt my life was surging forward. It was almost too much to contemplate. There was also the tinge of danger hanging over the whole venture. Our journey was rife with uncertainty, which added to the adrenaline and lent a kind of filmic vitality to the whole enterprise. This was terrible, really, because of course the war was horrific and anything but filmic, but still, that's what a lot of us younger ones felt.

EIGHT

ENSA

Early 1945

Pauline Clayden, Paula Dunning and me

WE WERE GOING TO BE close to the heart of the war, but the other young ones and I were below the legal limit for proximity to danger zones. This meant my father and Madam de Valois had had to swear before a judge that I would be guarded night and day. It was an almost cartoonish occasion – Daddy in uniform, upright and to attention as always, standing next to my revered boss Madam, whose grey fur was flung nonchalantly round her neck. They both stood straight-backed, looking up at the judge as he peered down at them from his raised desk. I kept out of the way in the shadows, feeling, I must say, precociously important for a mere minion of the ballet. The judge was adamant, as he must have been with the other teenagers, that Madam swear we would be protected at all times especially at nights when, he insisted, someone should remain on guard outside our bedrooms. The ENSA commander and Madam agreed this would be so, and Daddy pronounced his satisfaction with the arrangements. As they swung round to leave the court, Madam hissed, 'Now, Lynne, good behaviour from you, please – from now on!' and she smiled as she sailed past. Daddy winked.

Madam and Fred made sure that the programmes of ballets we were taking over to the troops were well prepared, with first, second and third casts in place, and everything polished because we knew that during the actual trip there would be little chance to rehearse. We had not been told our port of disembarkation, which was purposely shrouded in mystery. It wasn't just us – the mad, interesting ballet company – sailing off to Belgium that bleak January evening, but hundreds of troops as well. The whole of Europe was in crisis: Russian, American, Italian, German, English and Commonwealth troops all fighting flat out, sometimes pushing back and forth over the same five miles. The infamous Battle of the Bulge was still raging, the Red Army had penetrated into Prussia, V2 rockets were now hitting Britain daily and the Belgian frontiers had only just been cleared.

My goodbyes to Auntie Bess and Uncle Phil had been fraught as my aunt was nervous about the whole affair. Saying goodbye to Daddy had been a whole lot easier – he and I had been through worse and now I was becoming a soldier like him (at least in uniform if not in action). As we were sailing with hundreds of troops, we couldn't help feeling part of the Forces, especially as now we were in khaki and eating the same food, even though our armour was only entertainment.

We finally set sail from Tilbury in bitterly cold conditions, all wearing our new ENSA uniforms, scarves and gloves, late on 22 January 1945.

ENSA, 1945

23 January 1945
Got up at six, washed and had breakfast in the wardroom at 6.30. Went up on deck before but all was dark and I could only see the lights of the convoy. After brekker came on deck and suddenly saw we were only 500 yards from land.

Wonderful feeling. Slipped slowly into port and disembarked about 9.30 with all the soldiers. We were marched to lorries and were taken the short way into Ostend to a lovely hotel for breakfast. Then we roamed the town and had tea at the NAAFI with about 300 soldiers. Taken in lorries to train which we boarded at 3.30 eight of us in the small carriage and set off to Brussels. The train got packed with civilians and in the end we were thirteen in the carriage and we didn't all have seats. Journey didn't finish till 12.30 at night as the piston broke halfway and it took time to mend. It was a nightmare journey and we all thought we'd pass out. I have never seen the company look so ill. When we finally arrived in Brussels we were marched across a lovely snow-clad square into a wonderfully luxurious hotel. We dumped our luggage outside the dining room and then after supper we tumbled into our allotted beds tired but incredibly happy.

During our weeks in war-torn Europe, a poor private was ordered to stand on duty outside my room at night. In Brussels he was a boy called John. I would find my way to the hotel kitchens and get them to make, 'Chocolat chaud, deux tasses, s'il vous plaît' to help make the poor chap's night less bleak. We used to sit on the end of my bed chatting, but only after he had looked under it and in every cupboard saying, 'Sorry, Miss! I gotta do this. Orders you know.' Which was not perhaps quite what the judge, Daddy or Madam had had in mind.

Moira, Mossie, Topsy and I ventured forth into the streets of Brussels with a mounting sense of amazement as we saw the lovely boulevards packed with shops that all seemed to be full of delicious things, especially so soon after the liberation of their city. We went into nearly all of them, gorging ourselves on new scents and perfumes, which none of us had experienced before. It seemed the most exciting place, the buildings so fresh and new to our eyes. The streets were packed, including a large number of our soldiers on leave from the front. We certainly did a lot of eating, but mind you, it was bitterly cold. Over Smith's bookshop there was a warm inviting café where we had coffee and scones, all for about eight francs. We were joined there by more of our equally awestruck company and the whole thing was so wonderful and convivial that Topsy and I kept being told by everyone to calm down.

We were overexcited, full of *joie de vivre* – and a bit much, I'm sure. Ours was an officers' leave hotel and we ballet girls were the only women there. We spent a lot of time writing home but had also found out that there was a huge ENSA cinema and, while the poor stage staff battled to erect our scenery in the Théâtre des Varietiés, clear the orchestra pit and unpack the wardrobe without the aid of electrical light, we were off seeing amazing films. Along with thousands of servicemen we had the great good fortune to see *Pride and Prejudice* with Laurence Olivier and Greer Garson, and *Double Indemnity*, in which Barbara Stanwyck was terrifyingly good at portraying a frightening woman.

Monday, 29 January 1945

Rushed to class and we nearly killed ourselves walking up a steep hill to the rehearsal room they had found for us. Nice class – good to dance again – then back to the hotel for tea. Out of the blue Alex [Rassine] told me I was a very good dancer – hooray!! Went to the theatre and as we were going Constant Lambert was emerging. He told us it was as cold as ice and we could see he was frozen – nose and fingers blue-tinged. We soon found out how true his information was. Took out rugs, thermos flasks and thick dressing gowns – Madam's orders. We had to start making up by candlelight but they managed to get the lights on early so then okay. When 'beginners' were called we were nearly frozen but when we got down to the stage it was even worse. I couldn't feel my feet or my hands. Jean could not get a dress for Sylphides, so Topsy had to stay off too. What with worrying about the formations and the cold (we had to shiver openly) it was torture; nevertheless we enjoyed it and it went down well. I tidied up during Rake and practised my French with our dresser, great fun! Madam broadcast a commentary on Rake over the Belgian BBC while it was on. Then Façade, equally cold and I'm sure I did it badly but I enjoyed it all the same. Was going to the rosin box just before the finale said hello to John Field. David was there and he said to John, 'Isn't she pretty' and John said, 'Yes, beautiful.' David fixed to take me out tomorrow. He was so adorable and I now feel really happy again. After Façade *he caught hold of me and took me upstairs – held my hips – so now I retire so very happily.*

If ever there was an overwrought, overexcited person, I was she. First of all, I was *not* pretty and never have been. Second of all, David definitely was adorable but he was wicked too, like so many men who are exceptionally attractive, especially if they are the object of adoration of a totally innocent but passionate girl. But he was still with Joan Sheldon, whom I liked, and I was *not* going to betray her however steamy I felt about David. But nevertheless David bothered with me. He was always trying to advise me, improve my reading – what little time there was for it – seemed genuinely to like my work and thought I had a special talent. He watched out for me and I literally worshipped him – not just because he was the most handsome Prince we had but because he really made me happy. He knew I would keep my passion for him under control, but it didn't prevent him from pushing things as far as he dared.

We presented a wide choice of entertainment while in Europe: *Dante Sonata, Miracle in the Gorbals, Façade, The Rake's Progress, Les Sylphides, Les Patineurs, Promenade* and Pamela or Margot with either Bobby or David Paltenghi would add a *pas de deux* from *Aurora* or *Casse Noisette*. I was in everything except *The Rake's Progress*. I enjoyed all of them,

David Paltenghi

but the beautiful lyrical movement of the free-style ensemble ballet *Dante Sonata* was my absolute favourite and I worked hard to try to make it wonderful for Fred, its brilliant choreographer.

The real treat was that we were to give two performances at the historic Théâtre Royale de la Monnaie, the Brussels opera house. It is a beautifully designed theatre, grand yet warm, and it was very carefully looked after in comparison with most of the theatres we had worked at in wartime. It had a massive, very deep stage, which felt good to be on. Its backstage was meticulous, bright and friendly. Each dressing room was painted white and had very bright lights and wonderfully crafted drawers for each person. I went down to look at the stage again in disbelief. It was the largest by far that I had ever been on or near and there was the most wonderful atmosphere about the place.

Later I was to discover that this heavenly opera house

had its own shoe shop where all the shoes for each production were made, its own scene shops, its own costume makers, it even had its own wig makers. It also had a restaurant – I won't demean it by using the name 'canteen', though that, of course, is what it was. It was what one dreams a great opera house should be and it has sat at the top of my list ever since.

It was all such a change from life in the studio in London, or Addiscombe Road with Auntie and Uncle, or the daily trains to and from work. Our social life exploded and we were meeting all sorts of officers from all sorts of places. Here we were in a great city in a world-renowned opera house, a treat for troops coming home from hell and something utterly different from the usual people in their lives. The officers longed, in the absence of those they loved and missed, to make a fuss of us and spoil us. We all got along famously as if we'd been part of the Army, and they part of the ballet, for years. The bizarreness of the situation swept all frontiers aside. We had enormous fun and I can only hope our totally different rules and personalities, and our joy in our surroundings, helped them forget the horror of the fighting zones they'd have to return to only too soon. And of course the older girls, who were in their twenties, simply had the time of their lives!

Our last night at the Monnaie was incredible. It was marvellous to see Constant Lambert – such an inspiring conductor who understood dance so thoroughly – standing proudly on the podium of an orchestra pit worthy of his talent. His exhilaration was written all over his face and he bore us all away on a magic carpet of happiness. The rapport between dancer and conductor must be warm and understanding and, if it is, wonderful things can be created right there on stage, to the mutual thrill of both parties. If it is not there, everything can go on quite efficiently and professionally, but the magnetism that changes the whole atmosphere and lifts the performance will never be achieved. Constant was *simpatico* in the extreme. He was a man who could talk about anything and we often used to sit at his feet and devour his knowledge of art, food, wine, history, women and, naturally, dancing. And here he was at last, where he should always have been if the rigours and restrictions of 'theatre in the war' had not prevented it. The performance was inspired for one and all. The audience – including some civilians as this Gala was being held under the auspices of the British Council and had been sold out from the minute it was announced, and hundreds of troops – went mad at the end. Even though my life had suddenly been filled with so many breathtaking and undreamt-of experiences, it was a night to lock away in my heart and be treasured and savoured.

This glory could *not* last, however, and now we had to face the journey to Paris. The trains were all in a poor state with no regular services or hope of any kind of comfort. The company had to split in two as no train could accommodate us all – fifty of us plus thirty members of the orchestra along with sets, costumes, stage management and lighting equipment, the whole panoply of a huge travelling theatre troupe (and the largest ever sent by ENSA to entertain the Forces). Most of the dancers plus their personal luggage were in the first contingent and we set off on 19 February, in the afternoon, and arrived in Paris the next morning. It was a thirteen-and-a-half-hour tortuous journey, especially if you needed to visit the unsavoury lavatory at the end of the carriage. However, Henry Danton and I managed to get a little sleep up in the luggage racks, in between swapping favourite anecdotes of Brussels with our noisy carriage mates. At Paris's Gare du Nord we were met by the press, before being bundled into lorries with our luggage and taken across the city to a cosy hotel, the Favart, in the square opposite the Opéra Comique.

Henry Danton and me at the Gare du Nord, 1945

The company took up the entire hotel, and Topsy and I were in a room with big windows, which opened out on to the bustling square beneath us and over to the Opéra Comique, another historically important theatre for us to get to know. After a rest and some tea I went with several others across the square to see *Manon*. It was my nineteenth birthday, and everyone shared the cost of my ticket and gave me very welcome gifts of money.

When we had arrived at the hotel there had been two weeks' worth of letters from home waiting for us. Supper in the Hotel Favart that night was deadly quiet as everyone devoured notes from their loved ones. I for one could hardly believe I was now in Paris and had seen the famous Opéra Comique in action when only the night before I'd been in a luggage rack travelling on an uncomfortable train through the night from Brussels.

Our theatre was the little gem in the gardens at the bottom of the Champs Élysées, the Théâtre Marigny. It was small after the Monnaie but it was very beautiful and had a rosy ambience, soon to be broken by hordes of eager servicemen, some of them coming to see ballet for the first time. I suppose that was the inestimable value of this tour for the troops. Up to now, small groups of performers, revue and drama players had been sent out, but this was the first full-blooded ballet company and orchestra. They had had films and solo entertainers, but here was the magical world of ballet with its classical music and young dancers and which, had it not been for the war, many of them would never have picked as their entertainment.

Our tour opened up ballet to a great many men who otherwise might have scoffed at it. And once we'd got them in, we made sure we got their blood up and created future audiences for our company and our chosen art.

We opened with *Les Sylphides* to a packed house. There was a big reception held in our honour where the champagne flowed. One night after the *Sleeping Princess pas de deux* Bobby and Margot had to take about twenty curtain calls and even then the audience didn't want to let them go. As I wrote to my father:

The weather is wonderful, like an early summer and very warm. The two weeks of shows we gave at the Marigny Theatre for ENSA were a great success and packed every night. The boys really seem to appreciate us and it is very gratifying to find we get the same enthusiastic applause from an entirely different audience as we do from the almost fanatical London fans. We moved to the Champs Élysées Theatre to perform for the British Council. It was good to feel as if you were working for England, showing what she can produce to the French people. We had a lot to overcome because they have seen the best ballets the world has ever known here and their own Paris Opera ballet is pretty good but – with pride I can say that we really have been a marvellous success and they have encored and shouted for us night after night. The first performance at the Champs Élysées was a grand gala attended by everyone from the British Ambassador to Noël Coward and

David Niven. We did Promenade, Gorbals *and* Carnaval. *I
was thrilled because Madam chose me to do the Merveilleuses
in* Promenade. *The performances went very well indeed. Mr
Coward said to me how good Dante is!*

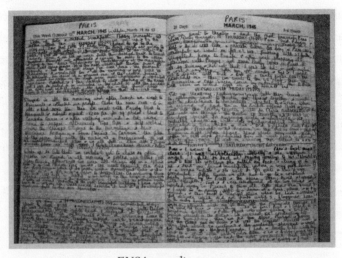

ENSA tour diary, 1945

Mr Noël Coward was just as intriguing as we had all heard.
He was one of the few men in English performing arts who
could act, direct theatre, write lyrics, write songs, sing, write
plays, musicals and operettas *and* write and direct films. He
was also one of the most observant men I would ever meet.
He could instantly read someone's character and was so acutely
full of sensibility that it was as if he could delve way into his
or her true soul. I loved him immediately but, as time went

on, I was to find out there was also a deeply sympathetic person under that façade of brittle brilliance.

The two Paris theatres we performed at were very different, but I preferred the smaller Marigny. The Champs Élysées was very large indeed, and grand, with a gigantic stage facing a cold auditorium. There were three huge rehearsal rooms where we took class with the Russian dancer Olga Preobrajenska every other day. She was the most wonderful teacher and such a personality. Even at seventy-five she was still almost as agile as we young ones were. She threw herself around, doing terrific jumps, and was altogether incredible. Preo, as we called her, had faith in me from the beginning and from that moment on I would never miss a chance to spend time in her studio at the Salle Wacher on the Place Clichy. She was a dance life-source and I wasn't surprised to hear she had been a mistress of the Tsar when she was a ballerina in Russia.

Preo teaching in Paris

March 1945

In our mime classes Preo shows us all the scenes she wants
us to act herself and she is such a wonderful actress and it
makes you cry to watch this wizened little lady who has
been one of the greatest dancers in the world acting so
perfectly and with such feeling.

I find I can really let myself go with her even in the most
dramatic scenes and she has taught me such a lot. She told
Madam de Valois she is very pleased with my mime and that
I really felt it all from inside. And after our last class she
took me aside and patted my hand and told me I was 'très
bien et une très bonne artiste', *which I thought was the*
nicest compliment. I was photographed at Harcourt [Paris's
most renowned photographer] and was one of eight chosen
to do a show class for the Paris Opéra. Madam gave it and

Portrait by Harcourt, Paris, 1945

it was the hardest I've ever had with her – she had me in
the front row next to Margot and was very nice to me!

Standing next to Margot in class was always daunting. She was so perfect, in such beautiful proportion and so very musical that you couldn't help feeling like a poor cousin. The only saving grace was I had a very high jump and that redeemed me. She was also a darling and was always lovely to me, so despite everything she made me feel at ease.

On one of our days off a few of us had a special class with Preo – just Margot, Pam, Gerd, Peggy, Anne, Alexis, Moyra Fraser and me. Preo was so inspiring and was enjoying herself so much that she went on for two and a half hours, finishing with thirty-two very fast *fouetté* turns. We staggered home to lunch and then, buoyed up by our class, Peggy and I went shopping all afternoon. In the evening Tops and I met two officers and went to the Rothschild house and the 45 Club, then to Montmartre, where we saw Sacré-Coeur by moonlight, and then on to Dick's hotel. When we got back we made boiled eggs and toast and were very late to bed.

We were a hit at the Théâtre des Champs Élysées and during our time there met all sorts of French dance person-alities including Renée (Zizi) Jeanmaire, Roland Petit and Ludmilla Tcherina. They seemed very modern, very vital, and they made me feel very home-grown. Our performances seemed to be a magnet for all kinds of new French artists, designers and musicians as well as dancers and teachers – it was like receiving a massive dose of creative fertiliser.

We also performed at the lovely theatre built for Marie Antoinette in Versailles. Versailles was the SHAEF (Supreme Headquarters Allied Expeditionary Force) and therefore an extremely important place for us to show our best colours. The theatre was exactly as it was in her day, except for the addition of running water and electricity. It was decorated in turquoise and blue, with mirrors in all the beautiful galleries and what seemed like hundreds of chandeliers. We gave *Sylphides*, *Rake*, the classic *Pas de Deux* and *Façade*. It all went down very well and we were made a terrible fuss of in the officers mess before we were eventually driven back to Paris.

Topsy and me at Versailles

One day Margot Fonteyn decided that I must have a pair of pure silk tights and she took me along the Faubourg Saint-Honoré to a famous shop where they specialised in making them. I blushed when the man ordered, 'Les jambes séparent à la seconde' and measured me with his hand naturally going right up into my crotch so that they would really fit. When I went back to collect them a few days later they were so beautiful I hardly ever wore them, but slept with them under my pillow. Margot had bought them for me as a present.

Life in Paris was dazzling. Many famous artists came to see us – Laurence Olivier and David Niven were often backstage visiting. One night Noël Coward, by now my favourite, actually held a door open for me – what a thrill. We even added Peter Pears and Benjamin Britten to the list. They were in Paris to give a concert for the British Council and we saw Mr Britten conduct his *Simple Symphony*. For the older ones life was very exotic. Everyone seemed to forget how young I was and one night I found myself invited to a party for a man who looked like the film star Louis Hayward. He was famous for being extraordinarily well endowed. All the dancers, men and women, were courting him and buzzing around him like overexcited bumblebees. Gerd Larsen suddenly saw me drinking it all in and I was summarily packed off to bed. I never found out who won the prize.

Our last days there were very busy. Mossie and I had our final class with Preo and it was a tearful goodbye. I loved that little woman and would have done anything for her. She had opened our eyes to so many new aspects of dance, not least to make more of our mime, to delve deep into the meaning of the old classic moves and invest them with real depth of feeling and understanding. I vowed to go and work with her in my holidays whenever I could in the future.

The company had become famous, we had made friends with many charming captains, lieutenants, majors, group captains, some extremely handsome and all brave, and were spoilt rotten all the time in terms of evening meals, nightclubs and safe transport home. We had been able to buy feminine things like perfume, gloves, stockings and blouses, no coupons were needed in Paris. We had drunk in the beauty of the city and its architecture, and we had been appreciated by troops, French artists, film stars and musicians. I had got to know Margot, Constant, Pamela and Bobby really well, and no longer

With Margot Fonteyn

felt like a beginner in the company, and my special mates Topsy, Mossie, Moira and I had had so many adventures together that we had become even closer. We knew how enriching this privileged time was – I don't think our feet touched the ground except when on stage.

Our last night at the Champs Élysées was upon us almost before we realised it: *Sylphides*, *Rake* and *Dante* – boy did I throw my soul into that last one. It was the most exciting show, followed by a noisy and appreciative reception. David Niven was in the wings and the audience wouldn't leave. At least, I thought to myself, we had not let Madam down and the company she had created would be respected and remembered in that wonderful city from now on.

The chatter that night, with so many officers in Paris on leave and wanting to share their experiences with us, allowed us to stay up to the minute with news of the war. We heard that our Winston Churchill had met Roosevelt and Stalin at Yalta and that a huge Allied air offensive had been launched against the German railway system. I wondered whether our already unreliable rail travel would be worse as a result. There was also talk of an enormous push to deposit thousands of men east of the River Rhine, thereby pressing the western front nearer and nearer towards Berlin and – as we raised our glasses hopefully – victory.

We were off again, north from Paris by train, to the old town of Ghent in Belgium, which was so crammed with Allied troops we were split up – boys and girls – all over the city and accommodation for some was spartan. But, as I wrote to my father, we girls were okay:

Darling Popski,

    We are staying at the moment on the outskirts of Ghent almost in the country. It is a very modern house with thousands of windows. It has a large garden and fields all around and every minute we are not rehearsing we sunbathe with short-sleeved jumpers and slacks, on rugs in the garden. Ghent is a sleepy, happy town with old and new buildings mixed up together with old bricks of different colours, numerous squares filled with flower stalls and several canals with quays. We are staying here until next Wednesday and I can't bear to think of giving back our uniforms when we get home. Somehow one is somebody when one has a uniform but when you are in civvies you're just one of the crowd and all the amazing privileges one gets in uniform are gone. I shall miss riding around in transport – jeeps, lorries, trucks – and all the gay friendliness that goes on between people in uniform, and altogether life will seem rather tame. However, this expedition of ours will be one of my treasured memories as long as I live. You'd better get a store of throat pastilles in for me because the first days I am back I just shan't be able to stop talking for a moment. I shall be most upset if you are away when I arrive because we shall probably only have about three or four days off before we start work again and I'd like to be with you all the time if it is possible. I wonder if you could ask Auntie if it was possible for her to get a day off so that we can all have a celebration and a late birthday treat. Fancy having a nineteen-year-old coming home to you – it's rather frightening, isn't it?

We were to perform for five days at the old Koninklijke Opera House and heard that our shows had been oversubscribed. I thought, with these brave men actually wanting to come to the ballet we should put on extra performances for them but this was not the consensus. Ghent grew more charming every day with its cobbled streets, glistening canals and its mixture of workmanlike warehouses and beautiful old inns.

Just before performing *Promenade* on 26 March, Gordon Hamilton, our brilliant tiny Australian character dancer, who was playing the lead as the Lepidopterist, pulled me into a dark corner of the wings. With a glint in his eyes he whispered, 'Darling! Do you remember Geo, one of the boys from the Monnaie? He has come all the way from Brussels and begged me to introduce you, as you are his favourite dancer! He's there. Can you see him?' And he raced off for his next entrance.

Friends and admirers often stood in the wings during our tour, although in England it was frowned upon. Geo was standing in the gloom looking very shy but sweet. I said a quick hello to him but then it was time for me to go on stage. Gordon stashed Geo away so that he could watch and not be in everybody's way. Every time I ran past I tried to smile welcomingly and of course there's nothing like being called someone's favourite dancer to improve one's performance. Geo begged me to dine with him but I refused, offering only to see him after curtain down. I was pretty mean.

Having been turned down for dinner he insisted on a walk. We strolled up to the square and, to my amazement, he told me that he loved me, that in his eyes I was the loveliest dancer, and how, ever since the class we'd shared in Brussels when some of the Monnaie boys had been allowed to join us, he'd tried to see and talk to me and tell me how pretty I was, and so on and so on. As a result I missed my transport and had to wait hours for a lift from Margot and Constant. Geo stayed with me 'to protect me' as he said, and by now I thought him genuine and charming, although I wouldn't let him take me back in his friend's car to my lodgings. When Margot and Constant turned up they were sweet, cheeky about the situation, and we had lots of jokes.

I may have said no to Geo but I thought a lot of him for travelling all the way from Brussels:

He kept stroking my cheek and saying, 'oh, vous êtes si jolie' and asking me if I loved him. I've never had such a serious do in all my life. He was charming – that was the trouble, I felt sorry for him. He begged me to give him one

kiss. Oh my goodness what a kiss. I was worn out after it.
Oh dear, that's the first real declaration of love I've ever had,
in person I mean – and it was all in French. I certainly
shall never forget it!

The next day we all moved to Bruges, the Venice of Belgium
with its special, individual feel. Our next two ENSA performing
spaces were especially erected garrison theatres. The show in
Bruges was rapturously received and we were very moved. I
felt there was no way we could be good enough for the boys.
The sight of their very young faces discovering something that
was new, and which seemed to give them some happiness at
this dangerous time, made us all feel we literally could *not* do
enough for them.

We left to give our final performance of the tour in Ostend,
from where we would also leave for home. The show was
exhilarating – both audience and dancers were uplifted, and
the troops more than appreciative. Madam made a speech and
I thought the boys would never stop clapping. It was a heavenly
last night, not least because while everyone else was performing
Rake I had a close encounter with David. We all played Rummy
after supper and I went to sleep so my diary says: 'thinking
only of O' – my secret sign for David.

Our feelings were mixed about our return home. We were
longing to see our loved ones, but England was going to feel
very unexciting compared with our recent luxury and all the

interesting people we had met. On departure day we woke to dreadful weather, black skies and storms, and we heard that no boats could cross the Channel. Tops, Henry, Joan and I went to a little café for coffee and gateaux, and we all walked down to the quay and watched the local boats chugging about in the harbour. We talked to some officers and heard that everyone was very tense and excited as the Allies and the Russians were beginning to push into Germany. For the next few days we passed our time waiting in Ostend, going to the cinema, drinking and eating except for the stylish Moyra Fraser and Leslie Edwards who cleverly found another distraction – the Casino.

Eventually, on 2 April 1945, the news came that we would be leaving in two hours. We ran back to the hostel, yelling at the top of our voices and telling all Ostend we were going home. We packed feverishly, had a quick lunch and piled into charabancs, which took us all down to the port. The authorities first had to check that all were present and correct, and we eagerly awaited the two tank-landing craft that were battling their way towards us. There was no sign of Leslie or Moyra, however, and Madam's face was white with anger. 'Where's the loudhailer?' she demanded of the officer in charge. And as one and then another were hurriedly found she said, 'Call them immediately!' And very soon, ringing across the twilight from multiple loudhailers, was: 'Will Mr Edwards and Miss Fraser return at once to the company meeting place!'

Madam was *not* pleased and by now the two vessels were rounding into the harbour. They made it into port and unloaded men, lorries and mobile canteens. There was some exciting gun practice and we stood watching, open-mouthed, and saw the gun puffs in the sky. I noticed Leslie and Moyra sneaking into place while everyone was distracted. The disembarking soldiers said they didn't envy us, it was horribly rough out there. Finally we were marched into the bowels of the now empty ships before being taken up in a huge lift to the deck. Joan, Topsy, Mossie, Palma and I squeezed into a lovely cabin for four. As we set sail, we watched with somewhat sinking hearts the Continent receding into the distance.

Almost immediately the ship began to roll alarmingly – she was empty and had lost all her ballast when they unloaded the cargo – and by suppertime I was as green as a pea. Everyone was very kind. I could not force my supper down but was saved by a wise seaman who said, 'Come with me, Miss. You need air and a sea-biscuit!'

We sat together in a corner of the top deck so I wouldn't be blown away in the force nine gales and he made me eat the whole tasteless biscuit, one small bite at a time. It didn't help, but the minute I returned to the cabin I had a violent attack of diarrhoea and afterwards soon felt my usual self. After watching the loveliest blood-red sunset I returned to my bunk and, mid-Channel in a war landing craft, finally fell asleep. Eventually we arrived back in England, much the worse for wear.

NINE

VE Day

Mid-1945

Dante Sonata, *1945*

A s soon as I reached Addiscombe Road and saw dear Bess and Phil I could tell something was troubling them. When Uncle Phil actually made the tea I knew something really must be afoot.

'Sit down, Jill,' said my aunt, 'I have some sad news. Your Auntie Tossie has died. Sorry, darling, we all wanted to tell you but decided it would upset you badly in the middle of your tour and there was nothing you could have done to help her.'

It was a horrid shock. Tossie had been wonderful to me at the most traumatic time in my life. She had been a friend. 'How did she die?'

'She had a heart attack and complications from it. It was fairly quick, Jill.'

We sat quietly, remembering my aunt. Holding hands, Bess and I wept.

She said, 'Aunt Genie would love it if you could go across to Bromley later in the week and help them sort out her possessions before you return to work. She has left you some things in her will.'

Despite the news about dear Auntie Tossie it was lovely to see my gallant auntie and uncle and settle back into my small room on the first floor of their house. Bess had taken some time off work and, as requested, Daddy also arrived later for my belated nineteenth birthday party. He had brought goodies from his Mess and Auntie and Uncle had really tried with what was available to make our supper delicious. It was like Christmas as I unloaded my gifts and there was so much to tell them. It was a happy evening. We drank a toast to Auntie Tossie and then I fell into bed and slept for a long time. The next morning I said goodbye to my father, but not before I had noticed he seemed brighter, his body language was sprightly, eyes wide open. Clearly a lot of catching up needed to be done.

I was frantically busy before going back to work with the company, but everything seemed very flat after the Continent. I felt very down about Auntie Tossie; she had looked after me so well when Mummy died. I went on the bus to Bromley to meet my cousin Molly and her mother Genie, and we all went to clear up Auntie Tossie's belongings. The garden at Langdon Road had been etched on to my heart ever since I had watched the men returning from Dunkirk, and the unselfish way Tossie had given me her rations flooded back over me. Genie and Tossie had been very close and were quite alike; we were all sad. I stayed with my cousin and her family, and happily Daddy got leave to come for the weekend so we could all be together. While I was there, I inadvertently saw some terrible newspaper cuttings about my mother's accident, and the next day Daddy and I took the 146 to Keston and went on a long walk down the old familiar footpaths where the three of us had been so often. We needed to talk all the sadness out of our systems.

Just before Daddy left I put my hands on his shoulders and said, 'You seem so much happier than when I went off to Belgium. Have you perhaps got something to tell me?'

He laughed, we both did, and he hesitantly offered, 'Not really, darling. But Auntie Bess has introduced me to someone.'

I gave him a big hug, saying, 'Go on!'

'Well, there's nothing to tell yet,' he replied, 'but I'm taking her out for the first time next week. I'll let you know.' And with that he laughed, plonked a kiss on my forehead and drove off back to his aerodrome. In my room that night I was full of hope and anticipation for my father. If ever a man deserved to be loved and cared for again, he did.

And before I knew it, it was back to work. It was a joyous,

high-spirited reunion. We were taking class and rehearsing in the National Gallery as now even the rehearsal rooms at the Sadler's Wells Theatre on Rosebery Avenue were undergoing some much-needed repairs. We had all become closer – more interlaced – as a result of the tour. Rivalries and ambitions aside, we had formed a tight group; we understood each other's faults and vulnerabilities. Beryl had not come with us on our ENSA adventure because of her youth – she was one and a half years younger than I was – and must have felt excluded from this excited, babbling group, but we were all looking forward to a long season in our favourite New Theatre.

I had arranged to meet my darling Maggie for lunch and sat and talked with her in St James's Park until it was time to go back for class. Maggie had a secret, her eyes were wide with it: 'They have approached me about joining the company!'

We both whooped at the glorious prospect of actually dancing together.

I said, 'It will be a little tough, darling, they are not mad about outsiders, which you and I are. We weren't trained by them and we come in already moulded. But I reckon after all you've done you'll cope with that easily and your charm will win the day.'

We prattled on happily at the thought of what we might achieve and I made her promise she'd accept before kissing her goodbye and walking back to the National Gallery for class. As I was changing Topsy ran in and pounced on me to tell me I was down on the notice board – the deity that ran our lives

– to be one of the 'Red Girls' in *Les Patineurs* with Grey, and one of the 'two Principal Swans' with Shearer in *Lac des Cygnes*.

I was stunned. I could never have anticipated this leap up the ladder. Both the 'Red Girls' and the 'Big Swans', as we called them, were soloist roles and often used as try-outs for people Madam and Fred considered very promising. The very strict hierarchy of dancers was: Ballerina Assoluta, Ballerina, Leading Soloist, Soloist, Corps de Ballet, so it looked as if I had made the leap from Corps to Soloist.

I looked Topsy straight in the eye and asked, 'Are you sure?'

She said, 'Of course, silly, I went to the New on my way here and it's on the board as I said.'

I clutched her hand and thanked her for being the bearer of such exciting news. I went into class on a big high. We all danced well that day, from a subconscious wish to be able to show all we had learnt on our travels, perhaps. We hustled to the New after class and all the way I was wondering, was this because Preo had made it obvious she liked my work? Or was it Bobby? Or was it Madam herself – after all she was the one who had seen me dance Odette at the People's Palace and had the idea to take me, an outsider, into the company? Once we had gone through the stage door and said hello to the stage doorman who welcomed us back with a huge grin, we walked along the corridor to the notice board. There it was, in busi-nesslike typed letters, so I was forced to believe it. I had indeed been promoted.

Topsy and I enjoyed a celebratory tea at Lyons and I rushed back to East Croydon to give Auntie and Uncle the glorious news, telephoned my dad to let him know his daughter seemed to be on her way and slept fitfully, too happy and excited for proper sleep.

Moira Shearer tying her ribbons

I learnt an awful lot during those weeks. I had to get stuck into the 'Big Swans' with Moira straight away. It was a privilege to dance with her. She was so neat, elegant and precise, and I tried to temper my slightly wilder style according to hers. In the end we both changed to complement the other and Joy Newton, our ballet mistress, seemed pleased. I felt extremely lucky to be dancing with Moira, but was worried it might look like *Beauty and the Beast*, she was so very beautiful to look at.

What saved me was my line and my jump. And the face? Oh, dear, well it *just* got by!

Then it was straight into the 'Red Girls' with Beryl. We were pleased and thought our first teacher, Madeleine Sharp, would be, too. It was technically quite demanding and the score's dramatic concluding coda accompanies the 'Red Girls' spinning right across the ice (stage) from upstage left to downstage right without a break. It was fun, but you needed to be dead straight in your flight pattern, especially next to someone as unerring as Beryl.

Beryl and me, hand in hand

Madam brought in the extraordinary Russian dancer Vera Volkova to take some classes. She had seen how much we had all adored working with Olga Preobrajenska in Paris – and indeed improved – and on discovering that Vera had arrived in London to teach had grabbed her.

Before long we were able to move back to Rosebery Avenue for class, after which we would run through the 'Big Swans' and the 'Red Girls'. One day Vera was taking the class and Fred watched. I danced really badly, just a total 'off' day. I was sure Fred's good impression of me would have been ruined for life. Vera spotted my despair and took me aside to say, 'Don't vorry. It happens to everyone. Better next veek, don't vorry!'

I thanked her but went back to Croydon quite miserable. I worshipped Fred and it was the first time he'd seen me in a decent-sized role in one of his ballets. Of all the times for my technique to falter, this was the worst. So I kicked myself around a bit and then went shopping to cheer myself up. I bought two nice outfits at Renée's dress shop, one brown and the other ice-blue, then had lunch at Wilson's. I felt infinitely better after that and my recovery was complete when I received a telephone call at home from David, who said he was missing me. I recounted all the details of these ups and downs to Auntie Bess, poor suffering woman, who as always coped admirably with her niece's oscillating moods.

Our season opened at the New and we were welcomed right royally by the public. I was truly happy in my leading swan role. Mercifully, my technique was on form and my jump facilitated the *entrechats six* – feet crossing in the air three

times in elevation – and the whole lilting breadth of the choreography was rewarding to perform. Shearer and I felt joyous
with it – she was always very inclusive and we got on really
well, so we enjoyed delivering it as a twosome.

Les Patineurs also went well. Harold Turner, whom I had
watched in awe in the performances Mummy had taken me
to at Sadler's Wells when I was very young, had returned from
the RAF. He resumed the roles created for him by Fred,
including *Les Patineurs*, which had made him a celebrity, so
good and strong was his technique and so charming his personality. He played the 'Blue Boy' with a cheeky hat and plenty
of bravura, and was irresistible and sexy. The ballet itself was
a charming pastiche, Fred's beautifully choreographed observations of 'life on the ice'. Besides the 'Blue Boy' role there was
the 'Blue *Pas de Trois*', three tiny clever sharp dancers spinning
everywhere; the 'Red Girls' duet, a little more elegant but with

A fallen 'Red Girl' in Les Patineurs, *1945*

the fun of falling flat on the floor several times; and the 'White Couple', so glamorous as the pair glided across the ice in their romantic *pas de deux*.

Alongside all my smaller parts I was now dancing something special every evening as well, though I am happy to say I was still a scurrying 'Ant' in *Le Festin de l'Araignée*

It was such a fertile and lucky moment to have been part of Sadler's Wells. We had all progressed after our time on the Continent – with all the personalities, teachers, sights, sounds and general breadth of being exposed to different ways of life – but back in London I had the sensation we were sailing on a great galleon whose sons were returning to her from all directions, thankfully and with relief in their hearts. It was incredibly infectious and it felt as if we were skimming not walking across the earth.

Then the war in Europe was over! The whole of England took to the streets for Victory in Europe Day on 8 May 1945, celebrating the Nazis' surrender and the end of the Third Reich. Trafalgar Square was bursting with people cheering, hugging and laughing; you could not see an inch of pavement the feet were so tightly packed. The force of people's emotions made them cling together. That night we gave our three-act *Coppelia* at the New, in an explosive and original performance straight from the heart. Bobby Helpmann's Dr Coppelius was outrageous. He repeatedly brought balloons, decorations and flags on stage and wrapped everything up with a mad and memorable speech, bringing all his Shakespearean knowledge into play, from the Doctor's balcony at the end. Once the house had emptied we rushed backstage to change as fast as we could and followed the audience down St Martin's Lane, cheering and yelling with the best of them. The nation was bound together as one, a solid, powerful, positive, potently amazing force, unbeatable. It was a rare moment indeed and certainly one never to be forgotten.

Celebrating VE Day, with Frederick Ashton

On top of all this excitement another breakthrough role now came up for me. Madam and Constant had decided we needed another English composer of note to add to the list of chore-ographers and composers included in this important season, which would now be our first after the war. So to my delight they decided to bring back Fred Ashton's *The Quest* with its dazzling Walton score. Neither composer nor choreographer was totally satisfied with his work on this ballet, however, and it was not destined for a long life. But both men were so important on the English artistic scene that Madam and Constant pressed ahead with their plans, scheduling special performances of *The Quest*. They already had the set, an extraordinarily beautiful one by the great artist John Piper, and they had the score and orchestra parts. And what's more, many of the original male cast were now returning home from various Forces and could pick up their roles.

I had the good fortune to be cast as one of two Bats – evil spirits, henchmen of the evil magician. I leapt at the opportunity to dance the wicked steps with sharp little jagged jumps all *en pointe* with angular arms and head and all at great speed. It was a chance to show I could play nasty character roles and I revelled in it. I found the score wonderfully theatrical and it has these amazing gear changes in it, which are such a turn-on to perform – the score gave us all we needed to make Fred's work thrilling and effective. I knew I'd pulled it off because afterwards there was a transformation in the way Madam, Fred and Bobby looked at and included me. Fred was pleased and told me so.

Thankfully there were also more human roles. I seemed to be working my way up the ladder, getting small soloist roles and feeling my strength. I was one of two Ballet Girls in *Prospect Before Us* by de Valois, with two brilliant performances from Helpmann and Gordon Hamilton as rival theatre owners. It was a funny, witty ballet full of interesting highly etched individuals. It gave me a chance to show off and be comic. I continued to dance Fred's *Dante Sonata*, in which I now attained a front position, having worked my way up from the back. I could dance well in this because it suited my free spirit. 'Prayer' in *Coppelia* was also added to my roster.

'Prayer' in Coppelia

Auntie Bess and Uncle Phil came to see me in one of my wildlife roles – the Bat – and had a good time. The New is such a warm and friendly theatre when packed to the gills. We now had an orchestra with Constant in command of, instead of pounding the keyboards in, the pit. The company was looking good. We all went for a drink at the pub and then Mossie, Topsy and I took Bess and Phil up to one of the small cafés opposite the theatre. Food was still pretty dismal but that night we didn't care. We all talked, and talked and during the chat Auntie told us how exquisite she had found Margot's work. She too seemed to have grown out of all proportion during the Brussels–Paris expedition. Margot now looked like an international – not just a beautiful home-grown – star.

That night on the train back – what a pleasure this journey had become now that the bombs had disappeared – I asked Auntie about Daddy's new friend. He had taken her out on their first date and all had gone well, and I knew he really felt good about her. My aunt told me that Wilsie – a strange name I had never heard before – Kirby was a member of the famous Kirby's Flying Ballet showbusiness family. She had been the leader of the Grafton Girls, a famous group of English dancers who appeared exclusively at the Casino de Paris, working with Maurice Chevalier and Mistinguett. She and her mother had got out of France on one of the last boats to leave just before the war and now lived in Brixton. Wilsie was a strong but very warm woman with a huge sense of humour and she had quickly picked herself up and found a position in Etam, the lingerie chain. She had risen very quickly because of her spunk and intelligence, and was now one of their buyers as well as the manageress of the Croydon branch. She took the weekly takings to my aunt at the bank, which is how my aunt got to know her and introduced her to Daddy. Life was improving all round.

Maggie arrived to join the Sadler's Wells Ballet Company and I incorporated her into our gang as swiftly as I could; which didn't take long as Mags was such a darling and a stunning dancer. However, the hard work in the classes with Vera sometimes left me in despair.

Vera demanded a lot from me and I could not always deliver. This upset me terribly because it meant so much to me. It was usually Henry Danton who got me out of my bleak moods – reminding me about all my new roles, my new friends and yes, the now obvious flirting with David. When we finished the season Volkova made a point of having a quiet word with me – in her heavy Russian accent – at the party that was being held on stage: 'I know I drive you hard. Sometimes too hard.

Vera Volkova

But it is because I am so interested in you. You have a Russian soul when you dance. But that passion means you will have depressions when you can't be perfect. Just know how much I believe in you. But I will always drive you!' And she gave me a huge hug. I, of course, wanted to weep. How fantastic to have such a teacher bother with me so much. What's more, hearing 'Russian soul' from her was even more powerful than when Molly had said it.

The season over, it was time for a well-earned holiday. Daddy and I drove off to the Isle of Wight to stay in a small hotel where Wilsie would come to join us so she and I could get to know each other. Daddy and I loved the Isle of Wight with its wide sandy beaches, on which I could not resist dancing, beautiful green countryside and pretty thatched cottages. After

Me, Wilsie and Daddy, Isle of Wight, 1945

a few days Wilsie arrived and we got on well from day one. We had lots of outings and adventures exploring Bembridge, Seaview and Shanklin. One day Daddy took us rowing on the sea. It was getting a little bit choppy and he wanted to alter where we were sitting in the boat to get the balance right. In the process he fell overboard, getting his foot caught in the rowlocks. Wilsie and I couldn't help roaring with laughter and, as we struggled to pull him in, I realised she could be the one for him. Once we'd got him safely back in the boat, her affection towards him convinced me even further.

At the end of our holiday when we had returned home I said to Daddy, 'Why don't you ask Wilsie to marry you?' So he picked up the telephone and repeated verbatim what I had said. Wilsie immediately said yes. My beloved daddy's life, after so much sadness, was finally falling into place again.

Back in rehearsal we had an extraordinary autumn season lined up, starting with a week at the Finsbury Park Open Air Theatre. We enjoyed the chaos of open-air performing but were all very excited to hear that we would soon be going home to Sadler's Wells Theatre on Rosebery Avenue, which was finally ready to be reopened after the terrible damage it had sustained during the bombings. The whole building, theatre and rehearsal rooms, had been fully renovated.

At last we had our own, permanent Ballet Room to rehearse in and occasionally we even had the larger Opera Rehearsal

Room. Once we got into the Wells we sensed a swirling under-current of energy beneath all we were doing. It was hard to define but nonetheless it was there, propelling us along – it seemed that everyone was doubly alive. So much so that I started to find it difficult to sleep.

The season was full of new – to me – and very varied ballets and I had a lot to learn. *Les Rendezvous* returned, to my total delight. But even more excitingly *The Wanderer*, an abstract ballet by Frederick Ashton with music by Schubert and décor by Graham Sutherland, was in rehearsal. The older members of the company had danced it before but for the comparatively young ones it was totally new, and to me it was a revelation. Its mixture of classical and modern movement was like coming home. I felt every line and every swirl. Every extension and every free stretch sat on my body with ease and the music invaded me and made itself part of everything I did. It was fulfilling in every respect. One day Fred walked into the Ballet Room. First he watched us run through as far as we had got. He sat facing us all and, to everyone's surprise, not least mine, said, 'Listen! I want you to clear to the side and watch Lynne – she's the only one with the soul for this.'

Dance it alone? The shock meant I was bound to fall over. Margot, Bobby and Pamela were all there watching, and I went at it with everything I'd got, in spite of all the inner shaking. Everyone clapped at the end. Fred smiled at me and said quietly, 'Well done, Lynne.' And to the others, 'You see, that's how I want it done!' It was hard to believe that this was happening and happy though it made me, I was also very embarrassed.

From that moment on Fred watched me closely and when we opened the ballet in August the eminent ballet historian Mary Clark described my performance as 'one of great power and plastic beauty'. It was just my bad luck that this glorious ballet was only to last for a few seasons, but I had learnt what I could do well and that planted a seed.

As well as Madam, Vera, Fred and the rest of the company, two other important influences on my work emerged at this time. I became friends with John Hollingsworth, a young, very bright conductor. He was a very fine musician with wide interests and conducted concerts, films and finally ballet. It was good to talk with someone who wasn't a dancer, yet who understood it. I needed to learn more about music and John explained the intricacies extremely well, and talked to me for hours about musical content, structure and texture. The other person I turned to for advice was Celia Franca, who had been in and out of our company for some time. She was a very powerful character soloist – strong, fiery, a commanding actress – and she started to keep her eye on me and give me help with my acting and stagecraft. She didn't mince her words but I was so grateful that she felt my work had become worthy of her notice that I lapped up everything she said, critical or harsh, flattering or encouraging.

Despite having only just arrived back home, rumours suddenly abounded at the Wells that we might end up in yet another theatre. It seemed only too clear that the company would soon outgrow Rosebery Avenue. I thought the rumours must be true as Bobby had said to me weeks earlier, sotto voce in the wings, his eyes huge, 'We won't be making our permanent home at the Wells. I can't tell you where but it's certainly not going to be there.' So now everyone was restlessly picking away at where we might be going. These summer months were exciting but also unsettling – and very hard work, as usual.

The long season at the Wells came to an end in September and we left immediately for a three-week stint in Manchester at the opera house. We arrived in Acker Street on 16 September to classic digs: unappealing but snug house, a ferocious but good-hearted landlady, small but clean bedrooms. Mossie, Maggie, Topsy and I created a certain amount of havoc, dangling *pointe* shoes everywhere by their ribbons after their daily dose of hardening shellac, tights hanging out to dry in the bathroom and of course we shared two double beds. It was claustrophobic but fun.

The country might have demanded complete change by booting out Churchill's Coalition Government and voting in Clement Attlee and Labour, but rationing was still very much in force. At our digs we supplied the food – from our coupons – and our landlady, Mrs Dobbs, cooked it for us. One day we had invested our coupons in lamb chops. There had been a deal for five chops at the butchers, so we had one for each of us, and one spare to share. We handed them in to be cooked for our 'high tea'. We waited impatiently as the smell took over the house, the hard work of class and rehearsals causing anxious pits in our stomachs. We could hardly wait for the moment our landlady came in – carrying four chops. We were aghast and deeply suspicious. With no discussion between us we just kept her talking, even as we smelt the chop she'd kept back for herself getting more and more burnt. Only when we were sure it must have burnt to a crisp did we say, 'We must get on and eat now Mrs Dobbs – thank you!'

One day the entire company was called to a meeting in a very unlikely place, the Manchester branch of Lewis's department store, and a new authority figure entered our lives. David Webster was the head of the Lewis group and a knowledgeable lover of music, art and opera. He announced that the Royal Opera House Covent Garden, which had become, of all things, a dance hall during the war, was to reopen in early 1946 and would be home to the Covent Garden Opera Company *and* the Sadler's Wells Ballet. He would be the Administrator and Ninette would be the Artistic Director of the Ballet. It was almost too much to comprehend – a new home for our company in a ravishing, albeit run-down, opera house in the middle of London – and we were to open with a full-length new production of *The Sleeping Princess*, to be renamed *The Sleeping Beauty* and designed by the great Oliver Messel. As we dispersed the chat was deafening. On the whole, we were exultant. Of course there were a few dunderheads who were fearful but we had liked David Webster and felt the adrenaline rise. Wild plans were thrown about as we threaded our noisy way down through the store. We didn't even notice the gleaming kitchen utensils, women's lacy lingerie, men's chunky socks, underpants and shiny cosmetics; we were far too excited to notice how incongruous all our prattle about *The Sleeping Beauty* and Covent Garden must have seemed amidst all that winceyette and heavy flannel. Mr Webster's revelations about our forthcoming life at Covent Garden had also unsettled most of us. What version would Ninette use for our *Beauty* and who would be given big roles? I had never seen the ballet, only read about it and devoured pictures of famous Russians and Lilian Baylis and Madam's Vic-Wells Company doing it. Would she bring in extra people to swell our numbers on such a big stage? The performance that night at Manchester's opera house was one of the most electric we'd ever given.

Our English tour over, we had only four days to prepare for our second Continental tour, this time to Hamburg, Hanover, Berlin and Düsseldorf. Daddy was very envious of the fact that I'd get to see Germany so soon after the end of the war, but there was also much talk of the devastation there.

The euphoria of the last four weeks, ever since we'd heard about our Covent Garden opening, was soon dispelled. We lined up on the quay at Tilbury feeling like old hands now and, thank goodness, the sea was not having a nervous breakdown, as it had been on our boat journey from Ostend. The crossing was uneventful but the trains were another matter altogether. Again it was winter and all the rolling stock in Europe was in a state of disrepair so, although the war was over on all fronts, most public transport was still in a dire state. Our journey was interminable and cold but when we did eventually arrive we found our most comfortable hostel near the Atlantic Hotel. It would turn out to be a very fortuitous location.

Maggie and me

After our difficult journey we were allowed a few days off while the stage staff worked to get the theatre ready for us. I had managed to finish our English tour, deliriously expectant about the future, by trying too hard and injuring my right foot with a nasty ankle strain. It wasn't healing quickly enough, not helped by the freezing cold on the train between Ostend and Hamburg, and I was deeply depressed about it. Our miraculous company manager Bertie Hughes, ever zealous about our welfare, popped around the rooms to see if we were recovering. He found me in the slough of despond, with Topsy, Mossie and Maggie chorusing, 'Look at Dotty Dismal over there. She thinks she'll never dance again!'

Bertie instantly rose to the occasion faster than a double *tour en l'air* and said, 'I think we should all go to the Atlantic for coffee. We're allowed as we are special ENSA,' and he waited while we donned caps and coats before shepherding us the short distance to the hotel. What a hubbub was there.

The Atlantic Hotel was well built and designed, with a warm, magical atmosphere – *and* it was an officers club. It was full of officers who had returned from various fronts, fully aware of how attractive they were in their leather fur-lined jackets, some of them bearing very brave war records as well. The lovely spacious foyer was full of officers of every rank, a few ballet dancers and some well-dressed civilians all talking at once, with waiters snaking in and out among them delivering trays of steaming coffee. I saw Pamela and Bobby, who, not surprisingly, had found their way to the action already, and went over to give them a hug and see how they had fared on the train journey. The tall man they were talking to animatedly turned round as I arrived. Pamela introduced him, 'Jill, this is Major Geoffrey Gordon-Creed. Geoffrey, this is one of our youngest girls, Gillian Lynne. Lovely dancer!' I looked at this very good-looking man and became twice as alive as I had been two minutes before. He was very, very charismatic and his smile was devastating as he kissed my hand. Pamela saw my eyes sparkling and twinkling, and chipped in with, 'Major Gordon-Creed was awarded the Military Cross and has been on incredibly brave missions for the Army.'

Geoffrey said, 'More importantly, I'm hoping to come and see you the day after tomorrow.'

Robert Helpmann and
Pamela May, 1945

'Oh, God, I hope I'll be able to get back on by then,' I said.

Whereupon Pamela scolded, saying, 'Don't rush that ankle, darling. Dance on it too soon and it will give you trouble for months,' and turning to Geoffrey continued, 'Dancers never give their injuries a chance!'

I kissed Bobby and Pamela, looked at the Major and said, 'It was wonderful to meet you.' And resisting my impulse to kiss him as well I turned and went off to find my gang, trembling with excitement.

Mags, Topsy, Mossie and Bertie were surrounded by young officers; they hadn't wasted a minute. One of the men remarked, 'You've been talking to our hero. The Major is one of our stars. Somehow he makes all the hair-raising missions he has led seem quite straightforward!'

I admitted I had found him utterly charming and suddenly saw him threading his way across the room towards our group. Joining us, he whispered in my ear, 'I thought I'd come and find you.' And the day exploded into a blast of sunlight. As I proudly introduced my new friend, my depression left me, I forgot the dull ache in my ankle and we had a delightful time. I will never understand how he noticed me. I was one of the youngest and least attractive of our girls and certainly was not versed in the arts of female seduction and sophistication. He was wonderful with everyone and obviously hugely respected and highly liked by all the other officers. I could not go to class that afternoon as my ankle was still playing up so, at his request, I stayed with Geoffrey. Never had an injury been more opportune!

'He is tall and dark and very good looking, has a very county speaking voice, which is awfully nice to hear and is generally the sweetest person,' I wrote to my father late that night. Next morning I tried to do class, but the ankle swelled up and Geoffrey, who offered to drive Maggie and me there, took me back to the Atlantic where there was an army medical officer who gave it some care and attention at Geoffrey's request. We had coffee and lunch, and I asked if he would drive me out to Blankenees, on the Elbe, where he was stationed. On the way we passed the famous bomb-proof U-boat pens, which had just been blown up. By now I had found out that Geoffrey

Major Geoffrey Gordon-Creed
MC, DSO

had been awarded not only an MC but also the Distinguished Service Order – and he was only twenty-five. I was in a state of utter disbelief that such a divine man seemed so at ease with me. We had a wonderful day. He took me back to the hostel so I could bath and change, and said he'd return for me and take me to the theatre. I felt uncomfortable about being away from my work but I was enjoying being with him so much.

He picked me up in time for the opening of the Sadler's Wells Ballet. It was weird being out front, watching it instead of contributing to it. We went backstage at the end, but my intuitive beau saw how sad I was not to have been on and whisked me away into the countryside outside Hamburg, where he had commandeered – perhaps the war was not yet fully over after all – a beautiful house plus a nice old couple to look after it. There was a wood fire burning, *Glühwein* warming in the fireplace and the whole evening became perfect. We talked about everything, did not pause for breath, and as the wine and fire surrounded us with well-being I realised that, as opposed to the strong crushes I'd experienced so far, I was now, at this most unexpected time, falling truly in love. I had never found it so easy to talk on all levels with a man or to feel I could reveal my innermost thoughts and not be laughed at and, to cap it all, he was so gallant. This seems such an odd word these days, but it really was the only word to describe Geoffrey's elegance. We reluctantly drove back to Hamburg at about 2.30 in the morning and I went up to my room thinking only of him.

We had six more fantastic days together. I managed to get on stage twice – once for *Promenade* and the other for *Dante Sonata* – but it was a struggle. Geoffrey was there, caring and understanding and driving me everywhere in his powerful BMW. (He was not the only one. All the officers had commandeered cars; most of them sleek and very modern in comparison with cars in England.) At Heide we visited one of his field security units. A special lunch had been prepared and I began to realise not only how popular the Major was but also just how much he was respected. It felt very good to be his girl. We managed to get back to the warm, romantic house with the sweet old couple guarding it for two more late suppers. I started to appreciate how much Geoffrey understood my naïveté, he could see how much I adored and wanted him, but he could also see that, for now at least, my struggle with my mother's beliefs was winning over my longing to give in. We lay on the floor often, in the warmth and glow of the fire, very gently in each other's arms and I found out how it feels when your limbs become limpid with love and desire, and time is arrested. My respect for him grew as he was only ever gentle and caressing, never forcing the issue. I had to struggle hard to follow my mother's advice, though – I certainly didn't want to – and as these evenings progressed we grew closer and closer.

Leaving Hamburg was painful mentally and physically. I

wasn't sure if I would ever see Geoffrey again, though I felt sure he would fight for it to happen – he had vowed to come and see our first season at Covent Garden. Still, the whole time in Hamburg with him had been so magical that I wasn't sure it could ever realistically happen again. I knew I would never forget him and I knew we would remain in each other's minds, probably for ever, but everything at that time was so strange and uncertain that it was with a feeling of bleak emptiness that I said goodbye to him knowing that our connection had been real and this would always be kept in our hearts.

Our next port of call was the RAF Station at Buchenburg. My wretched ankle was still not right so our ballet mistress decided it was better to give it two more days. I was missing Geoffrey and the way he had made everything better, even my injury, and I was missing performing. That evening I got to the opening night party early and was welcomed by the commander-in-chief of the station. He showed me the magnificent spread of party food laid out to thank the company. 'It's been flown in especially from Denmark,' he told me proudly. 'Of course there's far too much here but I wanted it to be a terrific banquet for you all.'

After the last curtain call the company arrived, beamed with delight and descended like locusts. The Scandinavian spread was displayed on two long groaning trestle tables, and the speed with which it was devoured was incredible to behold. As I left, the commander was leaning against an empty table, his face a picture of shock and disbelief. I went up to thank him. 'You can see how well your wonderful idea was appreciated, can't you?' I said.

And in a small, distant voice he replied, 'If you had told me, there's no way I would have ever believed it.'

The next stop was Hanover, which had been so severely bombed and the fighting there had been so harsh that it was difficult to get a sense of the place as an entity, a city. We had to be billeted around the outskirts as there was very little left of the centre – ninety per cent of it had been destroyed.

I was shocked that I had not been aware of the depth of devastation the war had brought. I had been aware of the horror in England because I'd lived through a lot of it and had seen bomb damage with my own eyes, often daily. But I had not realised the extent to which this devastation had spread through Germany once the English had built the airborne fighting force that had enabled them to retaliate. It was terrible to see and, after the happiness and glamour of my days in Hamburg, I was unprepared for the shock.

Life in a ballet company is a long way from reality. The work and personal discipline needed to succeed at all mean there's literally no time for anything else, even in the midst of a world war. Selfish and blinkered, you train like Olympic athletes, surround yourself with music, do nothing but learn new works and rehearse, mostly with the same people, and then you all lay bare your soul on the stage each night. You eat, you sleep and it all starts again early the next day. This normal regime of ours had been totally disrupted by these ENSA tours and, through them, we were being exposed to entirely different people and places, and our eyes were being opened to what was actually happening to the world. I, for one, sobered up with a bang.

Cheer arrived in the form of the officers who came to meet us at the theatre, in this case the historic Herrenhausen. They were very young, had been through hell in the Battle of the Bulge and were determined to have as good a time with this visit from the ballet as we were to be cheered up. My ankle had improved and I was easing back into class and knew I'd be able to get back on stage imminently. We gave our first performance to rapturous applause. (I think if we'd read the telephone book while standing *en pointe* they'd have loved that too!) There was a great get-together at the Mess that night. Maggie, Topsy, Jean, Mossie, Henry Danton and I found ourselves entertained by a jolly captain and three of his friends, who piped up with: 'There's a beautiful racecourse here in Hanover, we have horses in the stables, we have to exercise them tomorrow morning and it would be our honour if you'd let us take you.' It was too tempting to miss and our captain had it organised in a trice and arranged to pick us up at nine the next day.

Bundled up against the cold, we left on our journey through the ghost of a city and out into the country to the isolated racetrack. The stands were empty, of course, and there was fog everywhere, but you could dimly discern the white rails and green grass curving off into the distance. It was as if the place were waiting for its lifeblood to arrive – horses, pounding hooves, people shouting at full throttle – but at this hour all was silent and still, quite awesome. Our captain took us to the stables and there were these huge, noble creatures – the largest horses I had ever seen – nostrils breathing steam across the cold morning air. Their grooms and our soldiers led us to the track and the men leapt on saying, 'We'll just warm them up for you!' And as the light grew steadily clearer they disappeared at speed off round the track.

Suddenly it was absolutely obvious that when they galloped back into sight they would offer us a ride, and was that a good idea? None of us wished to appear chicken, but the horses were enormous thoroughbreds – were we up to it? I thought of Covent Garden and our company's destiny ahead, and wished we'd thought a little more carefully. Our musketeers returned and insisted that we take a ride and soon Topsy, Jean and I were astride and heading down the track. It was exhilarating and I had just started to enjoy myself when I heard the sound of galloping hooves accompanied by little shocked cries as Topsy shot past, gripping her bolting horse round its neck. She hung on round a couple of bends but then off she fell, mercifully managing to free her feet from the stirrups. Our soldiers rushed after her. She was shocked, dazed and bruised, but luckily not seriously hurt, so they carried her back to the stables, where she was carefully wrapped in rugs and given a steadying whisky. She would be off for a couple of days, just as I got back on stage again.

I asked John, our captain, if he would mind driving me around what had been the centre of Hanover again before we left. I wanted to make sure these memories stayed with me and that I would never be so unaware again, in spite of the cloistered life of the ballet. It was a painful and powerful experience and it did the trick – I haven't forgotten it to this day. We left for Berlin, having made some good friends – John's Cornish family even sent me food parcels for a year until the impossible food rationing was lifted, and later he came to visit us in Covent Garden, bringing the memories of that crazy racetrack day flooding back.

It was unbelievable that we could be in Berlin so soon after the war, and extraordinary to be able to walk through the Reichstag, to stand before the Brandenburg Gate, look down the Unter den Linden, one of the most talked-about boulevards in the world. It was incredible and ignoble to be in the city of Hitler's triumphs and degeneration, to feel the extent of human blindness, the denial, the ignorance, our own staggering lack of awareness that had contributed to the terrible events of the past six years. It felt a very strange mixture of excitement and fear to be so close to all that horror and all that had nearly been. As I wrote to my father:

I've been taken all over Berlin by a Captain Mitchell in his jeep and the most exciting place was the Olympic Stadium built in 1936 especially for the Olympic Games and behind it is the outdoor stadium where all those mass rallies and torch meetings took place and where Hitler delivered a great many of his most spectacular speeches. We went into Hitler's box and stood right in the middle of the arena with the seats sloping up all round. Everything was covered with thick snow and the temperature was a long way below freezing. I've lots to tell you about Berlin – the Chancellery. (I have some glass from the chandelier in the diplomatic room and some iron from Hitler's armoured car left in the courtyard, also a Nazi iron cross.) We had great fun with the Russians guarding the building as it is in the Russian zone and they were most amused by our antics. Henry took photos of us standing by the German eagle that was up over the main door of the Chancellery – it was an extraordinary feeling being able to walk all over a building that only so recently was Hitler's private domain.

Ballet girls, Russian guards and Chancellery eagle, December 1945

We danced at the famous Theater des Westens, where I finally found my feet again. Working in this well-known theatre, with its history of ballets, operas and musicals and which had survived the bombing, the street fighting and the manic rallies, brought our life in Berlin strongly into focus. This city had been central to everyone's lives before, during and after the war, and being part of it now was like a powerful injection; going to work every day through its streets gave us a sense of potent immediacy.

I began to be aware of how much work I needed to do before opening at Covent Garden. The long journeys with their extreme cold, the distraction of seeing one ruined city after another, the parties with attractive men in the officers clubs, were not ideal for a disciplined dancer's life. Working at the des Westens pulled me up short and I started longing to return to the regular routines and requirements of work. Daily strict classes, working on my overarched back, one of the causes of my injuries, *not* drinking at all and occasionally getting to bed early would put me in much better shape, I decided. I still enjoyed going to the Reichstag with Maggie and misbehaving by dancing all over the forecourt – we couldn't resist it – but the professionalism of the Theater des Westens was a compelling influence, and just in time.

We were about to need all the stoicism and resilience we could muster as the company lumbered its way through many miles of territory covered in ice and snow in unmaintained coaches towards Düsseldorf. As I wrote to my father:

We had a hellish journey from Berlin to Düsseldorf. It took us two whole days and all the time the temperature was eight degrees below zero, the insides of the various coaches were iced over and we had only three proper meals in two days. Fourteen of us had the worst time of anyone. We had to change coaches six times as we kept breaking down. For two and a half hours we had to travel in an open lorry. I have never been so cold in all my life and thought I'd never get warm again. Everyone was wonderful all through, singing every song we ever knew, and when we ran out we sang hymns and carols – if we hadn't laughed we would have cried. We were made a huge fuss of when we arrived and are in a lovely hostel and we four, Mossie, Topsy, Maggie and I, have a first-floor room with a balcony overlooking the bombed framework of Düsseldorf. The whole place is warm so we are very lucky. Geoffrey is going to phone me here – if he can get through – so I am very excited about that as you can imagine. I'm longing for our first Xmas at home for six years, aren't you? Could we have a party – and can Maggie spend the second week of the holidays with us? I shall be so happy if we can be in our lovely little home – also if Geoffrey can come to Covent Garden and he brings me home in the car I shall be so proud to bring him to meet you at the bungalow – or anybody I may meet, come to that.

Düsseldorf was a skeleton, and the sadness was almost over-whelming as we saw the awful ruins everywhere. It would have been good to feel triumphant – after all, it had helped us bring the Germans down, this bombing – but the utter waste of it overpowered any such feelings. I found all the contradictions immensely unsettling, so I allowed myself to be saved by the knowledge that, at home, my father had managed to get things together and we were going to be able to return to our house, the bungalow, for Christmas.

Geoffrey managed to contact me in Düsseldorf and it helped to hear his sane voice when I poured out my distress. His total resolve about getting to Covent Garden was heart-warming. 'I'll help sort out your feelings once I'm with you. Don't worry,' he said and I relaxed, as I always did when I was around him.

We gave our performances in the badly damaged but patched

On the road with Maggie

up Opernhaus in Dusseldorf. In some terrible way the fact that the theatre had been badly hurt added extra emotional depth to our ballets. I was thankful that my ankle allowed me finally to get back on stage but, once there, I was aware of this strange brooding – a sense of things waiting to spring back into life, a density in the air. The theatre had been badly bombed two years earlier and it was as if it was glad to have something as full of life as a ballet company treading its hallowed boards again. I managed to dance *Dante Sonata*, the perfect ballet for this moody moment, especially as Fred had created it for the outbreak of the war, and my ankle got through it and life felt infinitely more promising.

On Monday, 17 December 1945 we set off from Düsseldorf for Ostend.

It was another long, cold trek but we were veterans by now, and when things became unbearable, unabashed, my gang sang, having learnt how much that had helped on our perilous journey from Berlin.

Finally we arrived back in Tilbury about thirty hours later. Then it was the train to Victoria before our rather subdued and totally fatigued group of artists kissed each other goodbye and wished one another 'Happy Christmas'.

Ringing across the platforms as the company dispersed came cries of, 'See you at Covent Garden!'

We could hardly believe it.

TEN

Royal Opera House

December 1945–January 1946

On my way to work

AT BROMLEY SOUTH ALL I could see was my father's gleaming smile, all I could feel was his arms enveloping me in a huge embrace. We hadn't seen each other for weeks and it was a moment of pure joy. My father had been very busy, partly with his regimental duties and partly getting the bungalow back to life and beginning to think about his return, after demobilisation was complete, to George Pyrke and Sons. We drove out of the station and down Sandford Road and then, there it was, our neat little house with a large grin on its face to welcome us. Daddy had found a housekeeper, the solid and friendly Mrs Mason, who was standing at the door saying, 'Who needs a large cup of tea?'

243

We both raised our hands at once and she turned and bustled into the kitchen. As we pushed into the warmth I collapsed – home at last. Daddy then introduced me properly to Mrs Mason, who was German but had been married to an Englishman for many years. She had a family but seemed happy to be with us rather than them – her children had flown the coop anyway, she told us, and her husband was away working. I liked her immediately and could see she was strict and had rules, which I felt at ease with. As we talked and the comfort of our home hit me I suddenly felt very, very tired.

'Bed for you, my darling,' Daddy decreed, 'and we'll bring a hot drink when you've settled down.'

I was more than happy to give in. Daddy showed me how he had made my old childhood room ready for his young ballerina daughter. There were warm rugs on the floor, a dressing table with drawers either side and a large mirror in the middle, a lovely wardrobe with space for shoes and lots of hangers, and a bed large enough for two. 'In case any of your friends want to stay,' he said, 'and I've got you a special smaller chest of drawers for all your practice clothes and ballet shoes.'

I nearly wept; he'd put so much thought into it all and he'd tried to think what Mummy would have done, I could tell. It had been painted a lovely blue with dark-blue curtains and the rugs on top of the grey-blue carpet were grey and coral. I had grown fond of my room at Auntie Bess's but that was in her house. This was in my house, *our* house, and I felt very emotional about it as I hugged Daddy and thanked him.

For the first time in six years, Daddy and I were at home again, together, and were able to start making up for the years that had been taken from us as a result of Mummy's accident and the war. I kissed him that night with all the gratitude a loving child could muster, and I fell asleep instantly.

45 Sandford Road, Bromley, Kent

For the next two days I lay very low, and was not my normal self at all. I spent the time talking on the telephone with Maggie, received calls from Bessie and Phil, and my cousin David, and a wondrous one from Geoffrey asking me to promise I'd always tell him where I'd be. I told Mrs M all about my German adventure and my feelings of distress. She was born near Hamburg and was upset by my descriptions but seemed sanguine about Germany's future. Otherwise, I did very little other than sleep.

Eventually I walked up the High Street and went into George

Pyrke and Sons to say hello to all the men working there and remember those that had not returned. Everyone had a story. Because I had appeared in the Bromley newspaper under the headline LOCAL MEN AND WOMEN ON BATTLEFRONTS: BROMLEY GIRL ON TOUR WITH ENSA they were up to date with all my news. I walked past the Bell Hotel and went to see if Madeleine Sharp was still teaching there, but she wasn't. I rang Beryl to wish the entire Groom family a happy Christmas and we agreed we must try to get Madeleine to Covent Garden when we had successfully opened.

Christmas Day at my grandparents' house, Shirleyhurst, was full of chit-chat and joking about the bombing and our time under the stairs, about my adventures, all Bess's bank news, the advent and joy of Wilsie, Daddy's military jaunts and the talk of demobilisation. There were such bubbles of laughter; so glad were we that we'd all got through the war intact. Uncle Sidney and Auntie Nita came over, he looking fatter, she thinner; both were being adorable. Grandpa and I went solemnly, and now slowly, on our traditional walk round the garden. We had a heartfelt conversation about Mummy and I told him I thought she would approve of Wilsie. We all had supper back at Addiscombe Road and eventually Daddy and I escaped back to Bromley, but not before I had thanked Bess for all that she had done for me and the love she had shown me. That night Daddy, to celebrate all that was to come, gave me my first fur coat: beaver lamb. I was very pleased with it but looked rather lost inside. It would have kept an Eskimo and his family warm.

With the start of rehearsals for *The Sleeping Beauty* looming I took the chance to go to the cinema, restaurants and concerts, and generally to enjoy London for the first time since the war. My cousin David got tickets for Noël Coward's beautiful film *Brief Encounter* with Celia Johnson and Trevor Howard, and I was reminded of the brilliance of the man I'd met in Paris and the enormous gifts of his interpreter, the director David Lean. It was extremely moving and the Rachmaninov score perfectly wrapped up the emotions the film unleashed in us. I also met Maggie for endless meals we should not have eaten.

Mags and I felt as if we were walking slowly along a diving board, the end and the blue water ahead, our stomachs tense with the thrill of the unknown. Maggie came to stay at the

Maggie, 1945

bungalow and we decided it would be a good idea to throw a 'Good Luck for Covent Garden' party. Daddy agreed, so we invited everyone for the Saturday before rehearsals started. We tried to get back into the swing of class but were delirious about our party preparations: buying prizes, planning refreshments, preparing a number that Uncle Phil wrote called 'The Ballerina's Lament' to perform as a party cabaret.

Finally it was the night before the party. We'd rehearsed our party piece and my cousin Molly, who was great fun and a giggler with striking curly red hair, planned games with us and painted cocktail glasses. Eventually we got to bed and as my eyes finally shut I could hear Mrs Mason and Daddy cooking and planning away in the kitchen.

We were woken early with cups of steaming tea and my father saying, 'I've just vacated the bathroom and I know there is a lot of hair-washing to be done, so who's next?' Maggie got there before me and I was thrilled with my extra five minutes in bed. I then got up and did a mini-barre and washed my hair in the bath. Maggie and I ran to Woolworths because we had forgotten drinking straws and napkins, and we bought a June-Curler because the very persuasive sales woman said, 'All young women throwing parties must have a June-Curler. It can tame the most uncontrollable hair.' Running all that way with wet hair had obviously made us perfect candidates!

Back at the bungalow, we worked out our complicated overnight sleeping plans. It was to be a full house, so with mattresses from George Pyrke and Sons at the ready we prepared the bungalow for the night's festivities. Finally, we leapt into our dresses just as Fay Thompson, whose mother had been killed in the car with Mummy, arrived. She had lived up to the promise of the very long colt's legs she'd had as a child, and was now a beautiful willow. I was happy to have her for a minute to myself; with all that sadness we shared, so deep and never forgotten. She was swiftly followed by all our ballet pals and relatives. Wilsie was the life and soul of our party, and Daddy was at his most charming and very happy, not least to see Wilsie fitting in so well. She gained total control of all my mad pals, making them laugh, leading the games, helping Mrs Mason, and she looked very pretty and vital in the process. We drank a lot, happily played and hungrily ate. Mags and I

Pamela May at 45 Sandford Road

performed our cabaret, Wilsie had us rolling about at her impersonation of a French goalie, which she'd learnt from one of the comics when she was on the same bill as Maurice Chevalier at the Casino de Paris, Pamela May gave thanks and spoke of the company's excitement as we stood on the threshold of a new life at Covent Garden. We danced, we sang – we had a marvellous party.

And as some people slowly went off home, we sorted our little house into a super dormitory for the rest. Henry, Stanley (Holden) and Malcolm slept upstairs in the attic, Topsy and Mossie slept in my bed, Mrs M was in the spare room, Anne Negus was on the sofa, Mags and I slept on a mattress in the lounge, Daddy was in his own bedroom and Nancy McNaught (head girl at my old school) was on another mattress in the dining room. Our bungalow was groaning with bodies sleeping peacefully in a happy haze.

The next morning we must have looked like a rather eccentric time and motion study. Mrs Mason and I stirred up saucepans of scrambled eggs and made slice after slice of toast, which we deliberately burnt as we'd all been told that charcoal was beneficial to us. As soon as someone emerged from the tiny bathroom they'd come down the corridor to us, pick up fork, knife and plate . . . and on. As the last one hove into view I rushed to the gramophone where my favourite records were stacked, got a lovely jazz sound going and everyone started to dance all over again. Eventually my father, fearful of ever getting his home back to normal, suggested that, as we had a momentous first day at the Opera House the next day and he didn't want to be responsible for tiredness or injury, perhaps it was home time. Sobered up by that thought, everyone flew into their street clothes and we walked them all to Bromley South station to see them off.

I wrote to Geoffrey in Germany telling him what he had missed, Daddy rang Wilsie to see if she had recovered, Maggie and I stacked the mattresses and prepared our practice clothes and finally went to bed.

Going up on the train the next morning I was very restless with a jumble of mixed emotions. First of all Maggie had come to the end of her stay with us and would return to her guardian on Avenue Road now we were working in London. I was going to miss her. Second, as we neared Victoria, I realised I was feeling sick with anticipation. Third, the casting. It was mostly a dark secret, except, of course, that Margot would be Aurora and Bobby her Prince. I was longing to see Margot again; she hadn't been to Germany with us and I knew she'd be in the pink. I feared that because of my ankle I might be left very much on the sidelines. As Maggie and I walked for the first time along Floral Street to the stage door of the Opera House I was such a mixture of excitement and nerves I almost hopped down the street.

However, it was great to walk through the stage door knowing that I belonged, and there were so many company members hovering about that the nerves were calmed and curiosity now took over. I breezily said 'Hello!' to Mr Jackson, the stage doorman, and followed the crowd along the corridor to the notice board to find out what the day had in store for us.

The Opera House was shabby still. The planned refurbishment to bring it back to its former glory after its war years as a dance hall had very much concentrated on the front of house, naturally so. The rest was subdued in colour and not at all plush, but to me it seemed like heaven and I had to pinch myself that I was actually in such a famous theatre, and that I was going to dance there. I wandered away from the others, down corridors and to the ensemble dressing rooms and the steps leading up to the stage, and quite forgot the notice board. Eventually I found my way back and suddenly 7 January 1946 became another of my red-letter days, for clearly typed it read: 'Prologue: Six Fairies – Shearer, Lynne, Negus, Clayden, Dale, Grey' in that order. I was to be the Fairy of the Enchanted Garden. Henry was to be my Cavalier and I had my own little page. What a thrilling surprise! I had never dreamed of getting a solo – my first with Sadler's Wells – on the opening night. I had to read the notice several times to be sure, it was the most wonderful chance I could have been given. I found Henry in the scrum and we hugged each other. No words were needed.

We were all called to the stage for class at ten and suddenly realised how vast it was and that we'd have to 'dance big' to cover it and reach out into the depths of the auditorium, which seemed miles away. We also discovered that the floor of the stage was quite difficult, it had patterns within the wood; some sections were vertical and some horizontal, and the joins were very occasionally a little slack. You didn't want to get your *pointe* shoe stuck in a crack for a pirouette.

The Sleeping Princess, first staged for the theatre in Russia in 1890, was a Marius Petipa and Tchaikovsky ballet, and one of the most famous classical ballets of all time. When Diaghilev brought his thrilling Ballets Russes to London in 1921, the ballet was staged by Nicolai Serguëeff. It was on this production that de Valois wanted to base our new one, changing its name to *The Sleeping Beauty*. It was a bold and imaginative step, as befitted her aspirations for our company's move to Covent Garden. And it worked: *The Sleeping Beauty* is how the ballet is known to this day.

After the first class Madam and our ballet mistress Joy taught the Fairies and Cavaliers their arrival and *pas de deux* work and dances. I revelled in every minute of it and felt like a mini-ballerina: very proud and very lucky. Moira and I learnt our solos, and Madam came and rehearsed us detail by meticulous detail. She was very sweet. I think she was as happy as we were to be working on that stage and all it promised.

At the end of rehearsal I went past the notice board once more, just in case anything had changed, even though I'd just been rehearsing the role with Madam. There it still was, in black and white.

Next day it was class again at ten with Harold Turner who,

because he was such a good dancer himself, always taught expansive movement in his classes, which was perfect for teaching how to cover that stage. Running through the 'Fairies' solos' was nerve-racking – there were a lot of people watching and I didn't feel ready to perform in front of such a critical group. I became acutely aware of the huge amount of extra work I would need to put in, not only to fill that stage but the auditorium as well. I realised my limbs would have to be absolutely sure and stretched to their utmost if they were to send out energy into that space; it was sobering.

On the way out of the stage door Mr Jackson said there was a letter for me. It had a German stamp on and my heart leapt. In it, my darling Geoffrey announced he had put in for leave and promised to take me on a beat around London as soon as his request was granted. Life was good: the Fairies *and* a letter from the man I was longing to see!

On our third day at Covent Garden a heavenly creature appeared, fresh from Moscow. Her married name was Violetta Elvin, but she was really called Prokhorova. She had the longest legs and the highest insteps I'd ever seen, making for a brilliant demi *plié*. She was also extremely pretty. She made me feel like a leg of ham she was so good. So I killed myself to be the best I'd ever been. We rehearsed the Prologue on stage with Peggy van Praagh. The work with all six couples was exhilarating, the music gorgeous.

The Prologue is very theatrical and exciting, full of drama

and with interesting and varied choreography. The King and Queen are throwing a grand christening party to celebrate the birth of their baby daughter Aurora. They have invited the six good fairies and each one brings a gift, carried by her little page, and is accompanied by a handsome cavalier to partner her. First comes the Crystal Fountain Fairy, accompanied by light, delicate and shimmering music; second is the Fairy of the Enchanted Garden (me), with fast busy music; the Fairy of the Woodland Glades comes third, with gentler, fuller music; then the Fairy of the Song Birds, with darting fast music very apt for bird flight; then the Fairy of the Golden Vine with more fast, exciting music and a solo named the 'finger variation' because of its sharp body twists accompanied by pointed darting fingers; and last of all comes the beautiful and serene leader of the Fairies, the Lilac Fairy, with sweeping, slightly grandiose music to suit her supreme importance to the story. Each fairy delivers her solo and this leads to the start of the glorious coda when the court is disrupted by the arrival of Carabosse, the wicked uninvited Fairy, who bursts on to the stage in her chariot and proceeds to cast an evil spell over the baby Princess. Horror and fear abounds as Carabosse decrees the Princess will prick her finger on a spindle and die. However, the Lilac Fairy confronts the evil and in a beautiful mimed scene she proclaims the Princess will *not* die but instead will fall into a deep sleep from which, one day, she will be awakened by the kiss of a Prince. To be rehearsing my first solo for the company in this

Lilac Fairy with David Paltenghi, 1946

scene gave me a huge incentive to work and every day there were new obstacles to overcome.

We were two weeks into our seven-week rehearsal period when I found out – oh, joy of joys – that I was to understudy Beryl's Lilac Fairy. Beryl was understudying Aurora and would almost certainly be called on to dance that role after we had opened, so that meant I was sure to be the Lilac Fairy, and soon.

We rehearsed the 'Floral Dance', as it was known in *The Sleeping Princess*, now renamed the 'Garland Dance' in our *Sleeping Beauty*. Fred was lovely and warm and encouraging. He was re-choreographing the old stilted Russian corps de ballet dance.

That evening I rushed down to Selhurst where my aunt met me and we went off to see Mr Jones, the osteopath. My ankle was still not fully recovered and I was determined it shouldn't get in my way at this crucial time. He got me on his table and after a long examination pronounced I had a bone out. He worked at it, I grimaced with the enormous pain, and he clicked it back, massaged my leg and strapped it. I hoped he was right and that now the ankle would finally settle down. I was tired so I stayed in my old room at Auntie's feeling desperate at this setback, and at such a time.

The next day I only did barre work in class as my whole leg felt stiff and after a quick lunch with Mags, Moira and I went to the great costumier Alec Shanks for a fitting. As he was one of the most important makers of costumes for the theatre in London, his rooms were crammed with costumes from past and present productions hanging on rails in every corridor and room. Moira's was finished and needed very little work. She soon left, waving goodbye to me as I stood in the middle of the very busy dressmaker's studio, on a minute wooden dais, in only a teeny pair of underpants and stockings feeling a little exposed. I slipped on my basic tutu and bodice and waited for our genius designer, Oliver Messel, who at that time was at the very top of his profession. And there he was, in his studio, supervising even the tiniest detail. The Fairy of the Enchanted Garden's tutu was to be covered with flowers and Oliver drew the design on my bodice himself. I then rushed back to the Garden to rehearse the 'Garland Dance' and Fred gave me a lot of solo bourrés (runs en pointe) to do. Oh, my poor ankle.

The rest of the week was filled with classes and rehearsals with Madam and Harold, including some in front of the Arts

Council. I rehearsed the Lilac Fairy and Carabosse scene, revelling in the mime the Lilac Fairy uses to banish Carabosse for her evil actions. I thanked God for those invaluable mime classes I had had with Preo in Paris and felt very on top of the scene, especially given I was doing it on that huge stage.

Eventually Sunday arrived and I spent the day alone with Daddy. He had his own worries. Demobilised, he was trying to fit back into civilian life at George Pyrke and Sons. It can't have been easy. And I was worried, too, about the amount and scale of the work ahead of me. I couldn't help blurting it all out. 'Daddy, the work at the Garden will get harder and harder and the hours longer and longer. My foot will need care and attention if it is not to let me down and . . .' It was very hard actually to say it, 'And . . . I feel perhaps I ought to try and live a little closer to the Garden so that the travelling is easier.'

He looked surprised, a bit shocked, but also sympathetic. I forged on: 'It just needs to be a small room, that's all, and of course if things get easier I can come back to you and the bungalow instantly. But I seem to be getting some good roles to perform, we haven't even started the third act yet and with all the fittings and orchestra calls I'm afraid I might have trouble achieving it all when on top of that there are the train journeys. It is a lot of time in the day just travelling.' And with that I lamely ran out of puff.

Daddy thought for a moment and said, 'Of course! The answer is Uncle George.' Uncle George, who had always been at the heart of George Pyrke and Sons along with my father, happened to be conducting a liaison with the manageress of the hotel next door to St George's church at the top of Drury Lane. 'Leave it with me, darling, we'll see what we can do!'

Two days later, thanks to Uncle George, I was able to rent a room in the hotel at a rate that I could just about afford. (In fact, I have always wondered if Uncle George secretly subsidised me in this venture.) My little room had a small electric fire that had two purposes: one, to keep me warm and two, to be laid upon its back and used as a stove on which to make my supper. I bought a saucepan and a tray and my meal was always the same: a tin of tomato soup (I must have bought a tin opener as well), a roll of bread, a little margarine (still not a lot of butter around in 1946), a tomato and some cheese. The beauty of the whole situation was that I could walk home from the stage door of the Opera House, turning right on to Floral Street, left on to Bow Street, right on to Long Acre then left on to Drury Lane straight up to the hotel, which was on High Holborn. Little did I know that, many years later, when I had become a choreographer, this was where the New London Theatre would be built and I would go up and down Drury Lane to rehearse my show *Cats* for all twenty-one years of its glorious run.

I knew the Covent Garden opening was to be a big gear change for me and I knew I had a long way to go. Being in my room away from the family hubbub meant I was free to concentrate solely on that and sink myself into this opportunity, not being sidetracked by anything else. This is not to say I didn't love my father with all my heart, but this ballet life had started with Mummy and I wanted this great occasion at Covent Garden to be a kind of gift to her for all she had taught me in the beginning. It was very delicate and complicated, but somehow my love of dance and love for my mother had got intertwined and I wanted 'us' to be alone.

Fred had started coaching me in my 'Enchanted Garden' solo. He was good, and ruthless and helpful. I worked so hard I blistered my toes. With Peggy, we rehearsed the 'Vision' scene. I played the Lilac Fairy to Shearer's Aurora with Michael Somes as her Prince. Now I could start to build my own interpretation with groundwork from Molly, Preo and Ursula Moreton, our mime teacher, to draw on. It was so rewarding, so illuminating; I realised how much I'd learnt from them and I vowed again to try to get back to Preo in Paris as soon as we had a holiday. We left these rehearsals inspired and with our heads held high. The refurbishments were continuing around us and when we saw the Royal Box we went berserk, not because it was particularly beautiful, though beautiful it was with its red plush and extra gold decoration, but because it would soon house our beloved Royal Family. Somehow, seeing this took away all possible doubts – we were ecstatic and proud to be there.

Madam had decided that Pauline Clayden, Violetta Elvin, Julia Farron (all soloists) plus the upstart Lynne all had bright futures but she needed time to study us individually and sharpen up our footwork, and this became her mantra. 'Now, I want to incorporate some special classes for hmmm . . .' Pause. 'What can I call you, people who, with work, could get somewhere? I want to work with you and strengthen you for the months ahead.' Her eyes swept over all four of us. 'Now, it's up to you to grab this chance. I've put you on your mettle and I want to see results.' It was the same mettle as a firing squad's, except somewhere behind it was affection as well. 'Sharpen it up!' she would yell in her normally gentle Irish brogue as we attempted the impossibly fast exercises she'd invented. The catchphrase stuck and we enjoyed repeating it and mimicking her voice – behind her back, of course. Despite the mimicking, we were all excited to be chosen for these sessions, but even the girls way up the ladder from me – Julia, Violetta and Pauline – were nervous and viewed the honour with a certain amount of horror. All imperfections would be revealed and with only four of us under her gaze how would we ever hold her interest?

Sometimes the four of us were called for coaching classes together, often on a portable barre placed wherever we were at the time, but sometimes we were called for a totally private session at the end of company class while everyone else was on a break. Either way we knew we were under extreme obser-vation and didn't dare put a foot wrong.

The barre work was finicky and difficult in its detail. The portable barre didn't help, and everyone was fairly put off by it, but, as usual, I was so proud to be one of those chosen that all I could think was, 'legs work well, back try not to overarch, feet be fast and strong, I *must* impress her, I must improve right under her nose – maybe she'll really notice me,' and I didn't have time to grumble.

And improve we most certainly did, as well as growing to realise what an amazing woman Madam was. The de Valois-choreographed ballets were witty, unusual, inventive, as full of integrity as she herself was, and sometimes incredibly inspirational. Her work has remained fresh to this day, partly because of the detail and character she built into her ballets. She created good strong roles for her leading dancers to inhabit, including the Rake (in *The Rake's Progress*), the Black Queen (in *Checkmate*), Satan (in *Job*), the two theatre managers (in *Prospect Before Us*). Her eye for detail was second to none. And of course she choreographed to her strengths which, during the war years, consisted of a core of brilliant female dancers and a few unusual men like Bobby and David who were from other countries so not subject to military call-up.

That she could keep her company going in the middle of a war, that she could cope with the management and financial side of it, choreograph new ballets and revive old ones *and* plan tours and nurture new talent was staggering. And she even had a husband in the background as well – 'Arthur my husband' as she unfailingly referred to him. We had all long been in Madam's thrall but watching her now, pulling this fantastical endeavour together made me think how proud Arthur must have been of this brainy, beautiful woman.

ELEVEN

Dream Opening

February 1946

Fairy of the Enchanted Garden, 1946

O UR THIRD WEEK OF REHEARSALS ended at Sadler's
Wells with the unbelievable news that I was to be the
second-cast Florestan, performing the *pas de trois* Fred had
re-choreographed for the Ball Revels in Act Three. The
company had three choreographers, Ninette herself, Robert
Helpmann and Frederick Ashton – each totally differing
talents. Of these three Fred was the purest and greatest,
Ninette the wittiest and most character-driven and Bobby
leaned more towards creating theatre rather than pure dance.
Bobby was starring in *The Sleeping Beauty* as Carabosse and
also as Margot's Prince. As Madam was directing the entire

production, she called on her star choreographer Fred to bring some of the Russian dances up to date. It was quite natural for Madam to feel that certain sections of the Ballets Russes production had dated a little and she didn't want one minute of that on 20 February 1946. She called on Fred to revise those sections while she masterminded her restaging of this classic into its new home.

I rushed down to Croydon that night; Bess and Phil were extremely pleased with my news. Daddy was at a military evening so I couldn't tell him. Quite apart from this, I had felt odd all day. My tummy felt a little strange but I couldn't quite pinpoint why. Amazingly, I had started my first period. Everyone had pulled my leg for so long that I had reached nineteen with still no sign of it, and I had begun to fret, thinking I had missed

*Beryl in her dressing room
at Covent Garden*

a gene or that I was made up of weird innards instead of normal ones. In one way this new arrival was a relief, on the other hand I began to worry that I might change shape or develop headaches, neither of which I could afford. I knew Auntie Bess would be pleased as she'd been concerned for years, but now she just became anxious about how I felt and would I be able to rehearse and all those aunty-ish things.

The next morning I ran to the station as we were to attempt the first rough run-through at Covent Garden for Madam, Fred and Constant to see if *Beauty* was shaping up well on that stage with the right storytelling, dynamics and 'placing'. Somehow the news had reached the theatre (had Bess phoned and spoken to Joy, or Madam herself, and asked them to keep an eye on me? I will never know) for as I walked through the doors for class Harold ran across doing a double *tour en l'air* en route to get attention and picked me up into an overhead lift. He paraded me round. The entire company clapped. I thought I'd die and blushed deep crimson. When he finally put me down it was Margot who came to my rescue and told everyone to behave and by now I could see the funny side and joined in the laughter amidst lots of over-the-top advice from the girls.

Vera Volkova gave one of her gold-plated classes, it was extra wonderful and I, anxious to prove that period or not I could still cut it, danced especially well, even managing six pirouettes in a lovely turning step she devised. We had a tea break as the stage staff set up the 'Prologue', then staggered a little clumsily through *Beauty* with Constant on the podium conducting the pianist. The whole thing was thrilling – pauses, mistakes, scenic blunders and all – and everyone was elated. We finished at 3.30 and Maggie, Moira and I, happy and hungry, grabbed something to eat at a little café and then went to see a terrific Russian Exhibition at Dorland Hall on Regent Street.

My first rehearsal of the Florestan *pas de trois* with Gerd and Madam was exciting. She was obviously quite pleased with how the production had looked on stage so was in a very good and witty mood. The speed of the Florestan solo was no problem to me, especially after the coaching sessions, so we had a happy time.

Until, that is, I pulled a muscle in my groin during a class with Vera. She was at her most demanding and I was at my silliest, trying too hard. We then rehearsed all the 'Fairy Variations'. We had to wear old tutus to give us the feel. I was not going to admit the discomfort – which was considerable – and that was tough. I watched Fred rehearse Beryl's Lilac Fairy and tried to learn as always from his discerning corrections and ideas, but I was fed up that I couldn't be doing it upstage as I would normally have done. I managed to get an appointment with Mr Dempster, the osteopath, who found that my pelvis was out. The treatment was very uncomfortable and ended with the instruction, 'No standing about for you tonight. Go home, keep it warm and *rest*. I'll see you again tomorrow.'

Feeling very low, I rang Mags at home, who immediately

said, 'You must come here to Avenue Road where Auntie Min and I can look after you – hurry up!' Maggie was a sterling friend if ever there was one.

I couldn't do class next day and went dutifully to Mr Dempster once more. Again, the treatment was painful but there was already some improvement, for which I was deeply grateful. Daddy came up and drove me down to Bromley, where a friend of Auntie Bess's had sent us her sweet coupons with a note saying, 'For all the hard work you both do.' Amazing.

Now we were embarking on the last lap the atmosphere everywhere was electric. We were no longer able to rehearse at the Garden, which was utterly consumed by Oliver Messel's demands and the wonders he was creating. The stage was a sea of calico and vibrant colour, with the flats all laid out and Oliver moving between them gradually painting as he went. The unpainted wooden throne for the stage King and Queen was pushed to one side with rolls of canvas leaning on it and there was an eerie quiet of concentration as the painting process continued. Even though we were needed elsewhere for fittings we felt the wave approaching and were all being carried along by its power and energy.

At the beginning of Week Five I heard that I was to learn Fred's new ballet, *Symphonic Variations*, which he had already started choreographing. This was astounding news. There were only six dancers, it had a score by César Franck and was designed by Sophie Fedorovitch. Everyone knew it would be

unusual. It was Fred's passion and it was to be the first piece
of Fred's to grace the stage of the Garden after the initial run
of *The Sleeping Beauty*. The first cast was Fonteyn, May and
Shearer; the men were Somes, Danton and the young Brian
Shaw, the current apple of Fred's eye. Avril Navarre and I were
to be ready to become second cast and begin rehearsing it. We
started learning as fast as we could, discreetly hugging the
back wall of the rehearsal room.

Symphonic Variations, *1946*

It was a dream ballet. The work was lyrical and generous, yet
fast and technical, flowing as swiftly as the River Arun that I
had so loved on my visits to Arundel in the war. It was abstract,
yet with a strong emotional theme running through it. So there
I was, not only with my own role in *Beauty*, but with the Lilac

Fairy and Florestan to come and now the pearl: *Variations*, second cast. Everything gathered pace. If we weren't doing class we were rehearsing the 'Prologue' or one of the three acts of *Beauty*. Or we were in a fitting for headdress and wig or costume. If I wasn't doing any of those I was trying frantically to get to Mr Dempster or Mr Jones to keep on top of my frustrating injuries, and now the press were beginning to turn up the heat. There were photo calls of rehearsals, portrait calls for all soloists, cameras at most rehearsals, all sorts of interesting people coming to watch and Madam was masterminding it all with her uncanny flair. And we still had to rehearse away from our theatre – at the Wells or Holborn Hall. We were forever on a bus or tube, dashing from one location to another.

It seemed as if the imminent reappearance of the Covent Garden Opera House as a major force in London's theatre scene was igniting the city. Theatre in general was sparkling in the aftermath of the war. Interesting productions featuring fine artists were flourishing and though we were still severely rationed, and coupons for food, clothes and petrol governed our lives, it was as if the population was somehow managing to say, 'Oh! I can't be bothered with that,' finding new dresses or suits, going to delicious restaurants and leading oddly glamorous lives in the very midst of the deprivations. Shows by Noël Coward and Ivor Novello graced Drury Lane and the Palace on Cambridge Circus, there were revues full of scintillating performers, Carroll Gibbons and Douglas Furber were writing and playing to devastating effect, Walter Crisham, Leslie Henson, Avril Angers, Hermione Baddeley, Graham Payne and Robert Nesbitt, doyen of directors of musicals and revues, delivered one glorious piece of theatre after another, and of course the film scene was at its most potent.

On top of all this, rumours were emerging, creeping out of cracks, slithering under stylish doorways, being whispered from bedroom to hall to kitchen to mews that England's high society was busy preparing itself. Smoothing out its slips and embroidered silks; shaking out its fur jackets and boas; lifting out its dazzling tiaras (dimly glinting from lack of use and needing care); pulling out its satin slippers; edging out its necklaces and earrings, which had been hidden away during the bombing and for fear of invasion; shaking out its sleekly tailored suits; discovering whether its stylishly patterned shirts would fit; removing mothballs from elegant jackets and nicely woven socks; unearthing gold and diamond cufflinks. Women and men alike were determined that the premiere of *The Sleeping Beauty* at Covent Garden would declare English society was intact and unharmed by the war, and that the country had picked itself up, dusted itself down and was emerging triumphant after the hideous conflict.

Our rehearsals now reached fever pitch and we were still dashing between the Wells and Holborn Hall, and for me there were also surreptitious journeys to physios, osteopaths and masseurs. But if we were frantic, so was the indefatigable wardrobe staff led by Oliver Messel and Mrs Hookham, our Black Queen – Margot's mum. In these post-war years you couldn't go out and buy a bale of silk velvet, or the thinnest net, or strong shiny taffeta or the slimmest whalebones for the bodices of our tutus. Oliver and the BQ were raiding their friends' wardrobes for carefully locked-up and never worn shot-velvet or thick silk dressing gowns; they found feathers on early 1920s hats in boxes stacked away and pushed to the back of cupboards. Their persuasion was all but criminal – people couldn't refuse such a formidable team. Their staff invented all manner of stand-ins for real materials, using everything from felt and raffia to dyed cottons, coloured wool and catgut. They raided old opera cupboards, which hadn't been looked at all through the war. They found old sequins and crumpled, jewelled feathers and lovingly coaxed them back to life; they unearthed old belts, buckles and silk linings and persuaded them to take to the boards again. Through it all strode the redoubtable BQ, giving energy and encouragement before rushing off again to be a detective as Oliver tore out his hair over a missing silver thread or a much-needed piece of soft pink leather. She was resilient and resourceful at the same time as taking every care of her valuable, ravishing daughter. Margot was beginning to shine in a fresh and special way. She was developing the aura that any star has to build around him or her so that they actually do seem to be lit from within. The cliché is true. It spurred us all on.

Madam and Fred were finishing the staging of Act Three while Margot, Pamela, Moira, Michael, Henry and Brian, with Avril and myself lurking, were rehearsing *Symphonic* almost daily as well as *Beauty*, and I was practising the Lilac Fairy as often as I could, not just the solo but the extensive mime scenes that she performs throughout the ballet. Afterwards, I would go either to my little room up the street or 241 Addiscombe Road in Croydon or the bungalow in Bromley, depending on what treatments I had coming up the next day. Gerd and Harold were very kind to me and often took me back to their flat in Hampstead for a meal.

It was all wonderful, but being in on the birth of *Symphonic Variations* is an experience I have treasured all my life. It took some time to build up the stamina for this ballet with its seventeen minutes on stage with no breaks. After the first run-through the dancers lay on the floor panting with exhaustion and when they stood up, six wet outlines remained. But Fred always brimmed with ideas that floated around the rehearsal space enticing everyone to become fluid, receptive and fertile. Watching him sculpt three such contrasting ballerinas truly was to witness a great choreographer at work. Margot, Moira and Pamela not only looked unusual together – one dark brunette, one flaming redhead, one blonde – but their dance 'lines' were different and so too were their dance styles. *Symphonic*, however, was an abstract piece of ultra-modern classical movement in Fred's inimitable and excessively musical style, and in it all three had to move as one, while still keeping their individual personalities and delivering Fred's subtext – he always had a story behind his movements, even in something as abstract as *Symphonic*. Fred wove a web over these three women and their partners, which enabled all six dancers to move together identically, filling César Franck's cool and beautiful music.

I wrote a desperate letter to Geoffrey. His letters to me were constant, whereas mine were becoming erratic which, I told him, 'Makes me so upset because I think about you so often and long for you to get here, even if only for a couple of days but I just don't seem even to have a second to sit down and share all my thoughts with you.'

Our last week dawned. Our theatre was nearly ready for us, but not first thing in the morning. So those of us who were in the habit of going for extra classes more than often went to West Street, which gives on to Cambridge Circus and houses one of the great theatre restaurants, the Ivy, founded by Mario Galatti, as well as the Ambassador Theatre and a famous old rehearsal studio known simply as West Street where most of the important teachers of that time taught class. Vera Volkova's class here was full to overflowing and the small room could barely contain us all. The noise in the changing room was deafening as we all gave vent to 'the moan'.

'I can't get my wretched pirouettes in my solo sharp enough!'
'My legs are so tired and taut.'

'I feel sick with tiredness, not sleeping.'

'I can't feel at ease in my costume yet. Is yours comfortable?'

'I haven't got all of mine yet nor have I enough *pointe* shoes.'

'Vera's gone mad on *fouettés*, fancy asking us to do thirty-two to right *and* left today!'

But the mood was exciting and instead of feeling an outsider, as I once had, I now joined in at full throttle: 'That beautiful jumping step she gave and I didn't dare do it full out because of my maddening foot.'

Our last visit to Holborn Hall started with a lovely class given by Harold and I twisted my ankle *again*, and again had to hide it, especially as we were rehearsing *Symphonic* and Act Three of *Beauty* on stage after tea. That night I went home to Bromley and Daddy drove me to Mr Jones, who gave the poor ankle a lot of loving care. Maggie rang to tell me the dressing-room list had gone up and I was to be in Dressing Room No. 2 with Julia Farron, Jean and Gerd. I was totally surprised by this elevated position but I think by now Madam had come to think of me as a firebrand and probably thought that putting me in with slightly older and definitely more experienced girls might sober me up. It didn't, but I was proud and happy to be with them. They were all fantastic dancers and performers, and they tolerated my mad enthusiasm for *everything* very generously.

The next day we moved into our new home. Dressing Room No. 2 was bare and comfortless, with one window, a scrubby bit of carpet and a small basin in the corner, but no golden arbour could have meant more to us. What's more, two doors along was Margot's room, so I felt overwhelmed by it all. I had never dreamed of being so near our Ballerina Assoluta. We were also allocated our dresser Em, short for Emily, a shortish, loving, strict Cockney – perfect, in fact. We all took to her on sight and very quickly felt we'd known her for years.

For the Wigs and Headdress Parade, Jean had a wondrous tricorn hat for the Countess in Act Two and as she put it on in the dressing room Em said, 'No, Miss Bedells, that's not the right way round!' And she firmly twisted it the other way. An argument between them was about to ensue when the tannoy screeched, 'Everyone on stage. *Now!*'

So we all had to rush along the corridor past the old VIETATO FUMARE sign and on to our vast stage. We stood silently along the front as Madam, Oliver, Fred – with cigarette in hand – and all the other makers looked at us, or rather our headdresses, wigs and hats, from the stalls. Notes were taken, arguments about artistic details were had, and next, 'Right, Act Two!' boomed from the corner where the stage manager controls the scenery and lighting cues, and from where the performers are called to their places. At Covent Garden it was positioned downstage left. As Jean walked forward alone Madam stopped the proceedings by yelling, 'Jean Bedells! What have you come as – Napoleon?' Amidst all the laughter I thought, 'Well, there's going to be hell to pay back in the dressing room.' However, when we returned to change, Em quick as a flash admitted,

'Sorry, Miss Bedells, you was right.' And darling Jean gave her a quizzical old-fashioned look and laughed.

On Saturday we had a full-costume stagger-through during which Oliver actually painted by hand, into vivid life, the thin papier-mâché flowers that bedecked my tutu. I was worried that I'd look fat in the costume as it was hardly sleek with the added flower petals. My headdress, too, had flowers all over it. But that is how Oliver crafted his costumes, from scene to scene, making magic out of the weird resources at his disposal to realise his designs. It was moving and amazing to watch his total command and cleverness, making this huge production beautiful despite inadequate materials. Nothing daunted him, he met the obstacles with intelligence and talent and surmounted all of them.

In the evening it was Constant's turn. Hearing our sixty-five-piece orchestra for the first time was an indescribable joy; it was electric. It lifted us out of the doldrums of the endless stage and costume calls and up to the top of our inspiration, giving us back our *raison d'être*. It also gave Madam a small break. She was grey with anxiety by now and, not surprisingly, her famous migraines had returned. Painstakingly, we went through every scene of *The Sleeping Beauty* so that we could become wedded in our artistic endeavour. It put us right back on form and Constant was patient, firm and magnetic, willing the best out of us all from the pit.

Sunday was our last chance to rest, though there was much to do to prepare for the premiere in three days' time. It wasn't really possible to put our feet up, only to organise clothes and first-night cards (to wish your dearest pals good luck), think deeply about the performance and of course for me, there was also another visit to Mr Jones for a treatment on my blasted ankle.

Daddy met me at the station, smiling as always, neat and polished and full of love. How lucky we were to have such a close rapport; not all children enjoy such ease and friendship with their parents. At the bungalow for coffee I told Mrs M all about the trials, wonders and hilarity of the recent week, and gave in to a cosy armchair and the genial comforts of home, tried but failed to refuse a piece of cake she had just made and reluctantly gave her yesterday's practice and perform-ance tights to wash. 'But Mrs M, they won't be dry. I think I have to go back up to London tonight to be ready early for the dress rehearsal tomorrow.'

To which she briskly replied, 'Jill, I've got my own methods. You'll see they'll be bone dry by the time I've stamped on them and hung them on the airer!'

I'd had a letter from Geoffrey the day before in which he'd said he was doing everything he could to get to London the next week, so I wrote him a long, newsy, loving epistle, not stopping to think that of course it could never reach him in time. Writing to him was just like talking to him and I enjoyed it. Also, I had recently found out that Geoffrey wasn't just in Intelligence, he was Head of Intelligence in Germany.

Listening to my stories of our rehearsals and our long hectic days, and the frequent visits to different rehearsal rooms, Daddy came up with a good idea. I had told him how once *Beauty* was established, the Covent Garden Opera would be moving into our theatre as well – we would be sharing the building and this meant we would often have to rehearse elsewhere and dash to the Garden for the performances. We wouldn't have anywhere to rest, even for a little while, before getting made up and dressed and on stage.

'The answer is a single mattress,' said Daddy. 'You can keep it stacked against the wall, then if you get half an hour you can enjoy ten minutes each on it as a tiny nap!'

This was one of the best ideas I'd ever heard so we leapt into the car and drove to George Pyrke and Sons and chose a small mattress, rolled it up, stashed it in the boot and got home just as Mrs M had put lunch on the table. Daddy then drove me to Mr Jones, who had gallantly agreed to give my ankle its last treatment on a Sunday. Afterwards we went over to Auntie's for tea as she had thoughtfully and generously picked up a white dress I'd had my eye on in Newman's in Croydon for the first-night party. After our usual heart-warming and easy time together we left with dress and mattress for the Kingsley Hotel and my small room, dropping off the mattress at the Garden en route and hanging my dress in the dressing-room wardrobe. I thanked my father and kissed him goodnight. I laid out my crisply dry practice clothes for class the next day, packed my pink tights into my rehearsal bag, fell into bed and lay there going through every move of my work in *Beauty*. Finally, I fell asleep.

All day Monday we dress rehearsed, sometimes with stops, sometimes carrying on, sometimes being ordered by Madam to 'go back to the start of the act'!

Jean, Julia and Gerd were a bit surprised by the mattress in our room but when it came to the break before that evening's 'No Stops' dress rehearsal everyone was grateful for the ten minutes each we allowed ourselves.

Em was at her most domineering, monitoring this precious commodity. 'Right na, Miss Farron, please, lie down, stretch out and give in,' then ten minutes later: 'Right, Miss Farron, that's yer lot; Miss Larsen, get down now, please, no time to 'ang about' and so on until we'd all been able to stretch out and snatch this modicum of rest.

Henry, my friend and Cavalier, popped his head round the door to see if his Fairy was okay and got yelled at by Em: 'Out, please, Mr Danton! Come back later!' And he quietly withdrew after a lot of mimed 'Sorry. Rest time here' from the other girls.

Supper had been laid out on tables in the Crush Bar and we all piled up in our dressing gowns to grab some sustenance. It was a chance to see how spruced up the theatre looked, with its gold cleaned and polished, its red carpets hoovered and gleaming, its chandeliers sparkling. It all added to our mounting excitement.

At the end of the evening's run-through Ninette and Fred set the curtain calls, which is always an unsettling moment for both directors and performers, signalling as it does that a river has been crossed . . . but the other side is yet to be conquered. It makes everyone feel vulnerable. But the Fairies were each to have a short solo call, which I was both delighted and terrified about. (What if no one claps? What if they don't like me?)

Margot Fonteyn, Act Three
pas de deux, Sleeping Beauty

Margot and Bobby were of course quite wonderful. He seemed particularly at home in this vast space and showed off his ballerina as if she were the most precious jewel in the world, and Margot, looking incredibly beautiful, allowed him to present her at her most humble.

After the run-through David, with whom things had cooled

since the arrival of Geoffrey, was encouraging and helpful as he always had been and I was happy about that. He was able to go out front a lot as the way the different casts worked meant he was not on as the Prince until the second night, therefore he could watch us in detail and come back with accurate observations, which we would then work on.

The day finished with notes from Madam, who looked on her last legs by now but sounded crisp and succinct as always. We appreciatively climbed out of our costumes, yelled 'Goodnight' to Margot as we passed her door and, as I walked home up Drury Lane, I suddenly realised I'd forgotten all about my birthday. Our opening day, the rebirth of a significant opera house and *the* event in London that would see the entire Royal Family sitting in their box watching our stunning new production of *The Sleeping Beauty*, would also be my birthday. I was about to leave my teens and become twenty years old. It was a sobering thought and I snuggled into bed feeling very uncertain.

My final day's rehearsal was filled with last-minute nerves, frantic practising of pirouettes with Henry, snatched conversations with Margot as we were both at the rosin box, a lovely talk with Pamela who would be dancing Aurora on the second night but the 'Blue Birds *Divertissement*' for the opening. She was sweet about my solo, which she had danced often in the past. There were endless consultations between Margot, Bobby, Madam and Constant, four human beings joined at the hip, making sure the tempi were perfect. There was a terrific class with Harold and afterwards a run-through of the sections of the ballet that Madam wanted to give a last polish to. Otherwise it was talks with 'the gang' to see how Maggie, Mossie and Topsy were feeling, trying not to notice that messages and presents were beginning to arrive at the stage door, getting out of wardrobe's way as they went from dressing room to dressing room making their last onslaughts and adjustments to the costumes, starting to think about our outfits for the after-the-show time. Finally, there was a talk from Madam and Fred about what they expected from us, what they hoped for us, and news that at the last dress rehearsal that evening there would be a small audience to spur us on and fill the auditorium a little. Some of the people invited were hugely important to the ballet and great supporters, so they would give something back to us instead of just sitting there and watching.

We hoped we had ironed out all problems – technical, musical, sartorial – and now it was up to us, her company, to repay Madam's faith in us by using our talent to bring her vision alive. My gang and Henry went down the Strand and had a quick bite at our favourite Fuller's tea shop; we allowed ourselves some of their delicious coffee-walnut cake, which they had managed to put back on the menu, and even convinced ourselves that the sugar was much needed for energy. We all walked back up through the market to the stage door well pleased with life.

It was very rewarding to see a few faces in the stalls for our final dress rehearsal and actually to hear some applause as the evening progressed. Constant was quite openly beaming with pleasure to feel a real-live audience behind his back and we picked up on that – it was like a bush telegraph running right through the company – and oh! that huge rich sound from the pit, so persuasive and totally inspiring, especially after all the wartime making do. The company who were not on that night – understudies, second- and third-cast Princes and the like – rushed to tell us how we'd danced and raved about the look of the whole ballet, and by the last act there was a radiance in the air that infected everyone, stage manager, stagehands, dressers and dancers.

How proud I was to be part of it, and to feel so at home with them all. I couldn't resist giving Margot a hug on the way to our dressing rooms. She had always been so supportive and

Margot, Act One entrance

kind to me and now we all knew she was on the threshold of becoming one of the world's greatest ballerinas, yet she was still fun and funny, unassuming and generous.

We gathered on stage once the curtain was down and looked at each other with new camaraderie. We had got through our show with no disasters, and with the effort we had learnt to be more aware of each other. We had grown as a group, we had stepped up a notch. It was very moving. Then through the pass door came Madam, Fred, Oliver, Joy Newton and even Madam's Arthur-my-husband and many of the specially invited audience. They all seemed happy and very appreciative, and even gave us a little extra applause.

Just after sending us away with admonitions to 'rest well. Take care. Good luck for tomorrow. Notes and class at two,' Madam called me aside and said, 'Lynne, I must take you over to meet Edward Astley. He likes your dancing and wants to meet you.' And she introduced me to a short, jovial man with a wonderful sparkle in his eyes. Lord Hastings made it quite clear how much he admired what I did – he said he'd been watching my progress intently – and as I said goodnight, he kissed my hand and wished me good luck for the opening. When I returned to No. 2, I was sent up rotten by the others with much laughter and good humour – they hadn't missed a trick.

I rang Daddy to say goodnight and tell him about the evening, and when I casually mentioned Lord Hastings he was quite impressed. I fell into bed after a little quiet time talking to

Mummy, sharing my feelings and hopes for tomorrow and praying she'd be proud. I did not wash my tights as I had decided to wear for the first time the next day the beautiful silk ones that Margot had given me.

THE ROYAL OPERA HOUSE, COVENT GARDEN, LONDON, W.C.2
Sole Lessees : Boosey & Hawkes, Ltd. ; House Manager : Peter Wakon.

THE COVENT GARDEN OPERA TRUST

present

THE SADLER'S WELLS BALLET

UNDER THE DIRECTION OF NINETTE DE VALOIS

Principal Choreographer : FREDERICK ASHTON

Musical Director : CONSTANT LAMBERT

ROBERT HELPMANN	MARGOT FONTEYN
ALEXIS RASSINE	PAMELA MAY
MICHAEL SOMES	MOIRA SHEARER
HAROLD TURNER	BERYL GREY
GORDON HAMILTON	MARGARET DALE
DAVID PALTENGHI	VIOLETTA PROKHOROVA
HENRY DANTON	JULIA FARRON
RICHARD ELLIS	ANNE NEGUS
LESLIE EDWARDS	GERD LARSEN
FRANKLIN WHITE	GILLIAN LYNNE
ANTHONY BURKE	JOAN SHELDON
BRIAN SHAW	

and full Company

Quite a few cards arrived at the hotel in the morning for my birthday and Daddy, Auntie, Uncle Phil and Wilsie all rang up. I didn't feel like eating and sat on my bed writing good luck notes for an hour. My dress was safely at the theatre so I wrapped up my white silk shoes to go with it and on the way down Drury Lane I bought two irises to wear in my hair.

It wasn't until I'd gone through the stage door and came up against a wall of bouquets – Mr Jackson was nearly hidden by them – and received the handful of cards he gave me that it really hit me. This wasn't just my birthday this was THE DAY – the day Madam had planned so meticulously and fought so hard to make happen. I felt suddenly shattered and pushed on up to the dressing room with shaky legs. There were lots of cards and little presents by my make-up mirror and everyone was very affectionate including Em who, when she came in, was carrying a bunch of snowdrops.

Jean said, 'As it's your birthday you can use my mauve eyeshadow whenever you like. I've noticed you like it!'

As I sat next to Jean I had secretly borrowed it quite often, always taking care to put it back in the same place. We had a good laugh about that and I thanked her for her largesse, and then it was time for class. It was one of Harold's gorgeous dancing ones and Dimitri, our pianist, outdid himself. As always, hard work pushed the nerves to the back of my mind and by the end of it – with a lovely big jumping step, enjoyed by boys and girls alike – we were flying high and happy. As we girls curtseyed to him, as is the tradition for thanking your teacher, Harold pronounced, 'Not only is today, 20 February, 1946, a momentous theatrical date but almost as important it is also Gillian's birthday.' Everyone, led by Margot and Bobby, sang 'Happy Birthday' and the tears fell down my cheeks.

Madam gave us all her notes on the previous night's dress rehearsal and went over a couple of things she wanted us to 'sharpen up!'. She then made a very dear speech thanking us for our amazing hard work. She said she had watched us mature into what she believed was an international-standard ballet company and how proud of us she was. Then, blowing us a kiss, she left the stage and the first night was upon us. The theatre had started to be peopled with ushers, programme women, a few police – the Royal Family was about to appear, after all – and a flurry of last-minute checks were going on all over the theatre. The Opera House staff were out front, dressed in their special best.

There was not a lot of chat in the dressing room as we made up, too much was going through our minds. I duly borrowed Jean's mauve shader for my eyes, Em fussed about as she prepared the 'Prologue' costumes, plus two Fairies and one Queen, and then there it was, the inevitable call – after 'the half', after 'fifteen minutes', after 'your five-minute call' – 'Ladies and Gentlemen. Overture and Beginners please – and good luck everyone!'

We filed out after good wishes from Jean and Em, and went through on to the stage where an electric, subdued hush pervaded. Mags and I hugged and pinched each other for good luck. The Company was glittering and looked ravishing in their Messel miracles. Bobby was leering and terrible in his Carabosse costume, Beryl was tall, beautiful and serene in her Lilac Fairy tutu. She and I whispered good luck and felt Madeleine Sharp would be wishing us well. Then we heard Constant's tap-tap on the podium, the orchestra swelled into the National Anthem and we knew our night had begun. After the curious sitting-down sound that always follows the anthem our stage manager said quietly, 'Places please' and Henry grabbed my hand and led me to our opening position.

The Overture happened, the applause at the end happened but I was in my own world. My whole journey, which had started so long ago with Mummy's help and all the sad and thrilling things that had enhanced and assaulted me along the way, had led to this incredible moment, and as Henry led me out on to the stage to take my place my heart

The Royal Family, 20 February 1946
(Princess Elizabeth, Princess Margaret, Queen Elizabeth,
George VI, Queen Mary)

sang out, 'You are here. You have arrived. You are about to dance your first solo for the Sadler's Wells Ballet on your birthday.'

And I looked out at the sea of tiaras, necklaces, jewels all glinting; the furs and two rows of uniformed officers from the Army, Navy and Air Force; at all the eager faces. And as I turned my head a little and there in the box sat our Royal Family, King, Queens and two Princesses, I knew that this was what I had always longed for and that I'd come home.

As the six Fairies and their Cavaliers danced the oh-so-satisfying Prologue, our *Beauty* started well. The music was most inspiring, the choreography good, the connection between us was tremendous and the sight of the sparkling auditorium, presided over by our Royal Family, made it difficult for us to keep our feet flat on the ground. Luckily that was the last place they needed to be.

We exited into the wings and waited our turn as each of the solos came up. The Fairy of the Enchanted Garden has the second solo in the sequence and as I heard the introduction and ran on to the stage, alone, an extraordinary thing happened. The audience disappeared, the stage King and Queen disappeared, the stage itself disappeared. All I could see was Constant egging me on with a smiling face and there was my mother above and all around me, willing me to dance with all my soul, just as she had that night when I'd shyly slipped into my first dance at The Hallams six years ago.

We were alone, entering the world she had always wanted for me, and I offered up my dance to her.

Fairy of the Enchanted Garden,
1946

Acknowledgements

F IRSTLY, THANK YOU TO Peter Land, who has supported, corrected, listened, researched, inspired and generally been the best help any author could dream of. To my wonderful office, led over time by Karen with Carol, Richard and Rosemary, for all your patience and research. Maggie Crews and Jean Bedells, for aiding and abetting my memory. The lovely Henry Danton, Rachel Hall (Moira Shearer's daughter) and old friend Dame Beryl Grey, for all finding photographs, and to Malcolm Goddard, for shared memories. The Royal Opera House Archives, for their help. My heartfelt gratitude to my dear Christopher Sinclair-Stevenson for taking me on in the first place and giving me the courage to persist. Lastly, to my wonderful editor, Becky Hardie, for having faith and leading me on a journey I could never have imagined.

Acknowledgements for Picture Permissions: kind permission granted by the private collections of Henry Danton, Dame

Beryl Grey and Margaret (Roseby) Crews, the Royal Opera House archives, the Gordon-Creed family, the Shearer/Kennedy Family Collection, the Pyrke Family Album and Sheila Jackson's family for the lithographs of me and Travis Kemp in *La Petite Fadette*, 1943 (Chapter Five), the pencil drawings of me in *Les Sylphides*, 1943 (Chapter Six) and rehearsing *Lac des Cygnes* with Gerd Larsen in 1944 (Chapter Seven). All picture permissions have been sought but I would like to praise the work of a generation of exceptional amateur and professional photographers including Roger Wood, Edward Mandinian, Houston Rodgers, G.B.L. Wilson and Baron.